# New and Selected Poems
## 1991-2017

# ALISON CROGGON

Newport Street Books

The moral right of Alison Croggon to be ideentified as
the author of this work has been asserted.

All rights reserved. No part of this books may be reproduced, transmitted or stored in an information retrieval system in any form or by any means, graphic, electronic or mechanical, including photocopying, taping and recording, without prior written permission from the author.

Cover art: *Eros and Thanatos* by Zoe Croggon
© Zoe Croggon
Text © Alison Croggon 2017
Newport Street Books, Melbourne
newportstreetbooks.com

Published by Newport Street Books, 2017
ISBN 978-0-6480676-2-7

**National Library of Australia Cataloguing-in-Publication entry**

| | |
|---|---|
| Creator: | Croggon, Alison, 1962- author. |
| Title: | New and selected poems 1991-2017 / Alison Croggon. |
| Edition: | First edition |
| ISBN: | 9780648067627 (paperback) |
| Subjects: | Australian poetry--20th century. |
| | Australian poetry--21st century. |

Alison Croggon is an award-winning novelist, poet, librettist and critic who lives in Melbourne, Australia. Her poetry has been widely published in journals in Australia and internationally, and is included in many major Australian anthologies. Her first poetry collection, *This is the Stone*, won the Anne Elder and Dame Mary Gilmore Prizes. *The Blue Gate* was a finalist for the Victorian Premier's Poetry Prize. *Attempts at Being* was shortlisted for the NSW Premier's Literary Awards Poetry Prize and was nominated for a Pushcart Prize in the US. Her poetry has been set to music by several composers and she has written many libretti, including *Mayakovsky*, for an opera by Michael Smetanin, which was a finalist for the Victorian Premier's Awards Drama Prize, and *The Riders*, for Iain Grandage, which was named Choral/Vocal Work of the Year in the Australian Art Music Awards.

She is the author of the popular fantasy series *The Books of Pellinor*. Other novels include *The River and the Book*, a finalist in the WA Premier's Awards and winner of the Environmental Writing for Children Award; *Black Spring*, a finalist in the NSW Premiers Literary Awards; and *Navigatio*. She is also a performance critic, and in 2009 was named the Geraldine Pascall Critic of the Year. She lives in Melbourne, Australia, with her husband, the playwright Daniel Keene, with whom she is co-writing a new speculative fiction series.

Her previous poetry collections are *Theatre* (Salt Publishing 2008), *Torque* (Ahahada Press, 2008), *Ash* (Cusp Books, Los Angeles 2005); *November Burning* (Vagabond Press Rare Objects Series, Sydney, 2004); *The Common Flesh: New and Selected Poems* (Arc Publications, UK, 2003), *Attempts at Being* (Salt Publishing, UK, 2002), *Mnemosyne* (Wild Honey Press, Ireland, 2001); *The Blue Gate* (Black Pepper Press, 1997) and *This is the Stone* (Penguin Books, 1991).

For more information visit alisoncroggon.com

# Acknowledgements

Poems in this collection were first published in the following books and periodicals: *The First Stone* (Penguin Books, 1991), *The Blue Gate* (Black Pepper Press, 1997), *Mnemosyne* (Wild Honey Press, 2001), *Attempts at Being* (Salt Publishing, 2002), *The Common Flesh* (Arc Publications, 2003), *November Burning* (Vagabond Press, 2004), *Ash* (Cusp Books, 2006), *Theatre* (Salt Publishing, 2008), *Torque* (Ahadada Books, 2008), *World Literature Today, The Australian, Aquarius, The Age, Kunapipi, Meanjin, Moveable Type, Slow Dancer, La Mama Poetica, Modern Writing, Linq, A Parachute of Blue, Alsop Review, Atlantic Review, A Chide's Alphabet, The Drunken Boat, How2, The Literary Review, Prism, Quadrant, Masthead, New Music: An Anthology of Contemporary Australian Poetry, Salt, Shearsman, Thylacine, Agenda, Pretext, Bad Press5.x, Famous Reporter, Great Works* and *Overland Literary Magazine*. *Rising from Aquifers* was originally co-written with Sophie Mayer for *Cordite* and was published as part of Sophie Mayer's book *what the wasteland said*. *Mayakovsky* was written for the opera *Mayakovsky* by Michael Smetanin, commissioned by Victorian Opera and first performed by Sydney Chamber Opera in Sydney in 2015. Some poems were initially written as part of the collaborative online project Offsets, run online by Trevor Joyce. My apologies if any acknowledgements have been overlooked.

Huge thanks to John Kinsella for his generous and constant support over many years, and to John Leonard, who edited my early poems.

Many poems in this book were written with the assistance of the Australian Government through the Australia Council, its arts funding and advisory body.

# Note

I lost interest in pursuing publication of my poetry almost a decade ago, but since most of my collections are now out of print it seems timely to gather my poems together and publish them myself.

For *New and Selected Poems 1991-2017* I've chosen all the poems I care to remember. I wrote the earliest poem in this book when I was eleven, the most recent this year. Some, including older works, haven't been previously published; some have been published many times, in books, magazines and anthologies.

I decided not to order the poems chronologically, nor to divide them into sections that reflect their publication in previous books. Instead I wanted to create a new body of work that, like memory itself, exists spatially rather than sequentially, moving allusively through thematic, stylistic or emotional connections.

Many poems have been revised, but I hope this has enhanced them rather than altering their original qualities. Clearly the work has changed over the years, as different ways of thinking and making poems caught my interest; but I think I have always been the same poet.

Alison Croggon<br>
Melbourne, July 2017

# Contents

| | |
|---|---|
| The poet has no identity | 1 |
| Why I don't like being photographed | 2 |
| Ode | 4 |
| Poetry you never lied to me | 6 |
| Beasts | 8 |
| Quickening | |
|     I  Family Notes | 9 |
|     II  Love Poems | 14 |
|     III  Howl | 19 |
|     IV  Domestic Art | 22 |
| Emily Bronte | 26 |
| The Elwood Organic Fruit and Vegetable Shop | 27 |
| Amplitudes 1-15 | 28 |
| Poem for John | 51 |
| Ode to Walt Whitman | 52 |
| All Souls Day | 54 |
| A flower | 56 |
| Billie Holiday | 57 |
| Lindy | 58 |
| Chekhov in Sakhalin | 59 |
| November burning | 63 |
| The page cannot be found | 71 |
| After Arseny Tarkovsky | 72 |
| The Gift | 73 |
| Coma | 74 |
| Songs of a Quiet Woman | 76 |
| Attempts at being | 79 |
| Beginning again | 81 |
| Pause | 83 |
| Leaves | 84 |
| Cassandra | 86 |
| The Edgeless Page | 90 |

| | |
|---|---|
| Seduction Poem | 91 |
| Fairytale | 92 |
| Sonnets | 93 |
| Sonata | 97 |
| Angels | 100 |
| Failures | 101 |
| A unicorn | 102 |
| Names | 103 |
| On the First Period after Pregnancy | 104 |
| Small Things | 105 |
| Of prayer | 107 |
| Wars | 108 |
| Translations from Nowhere | 109 |
| Pain | 122 |
| Colours | 123 |
| Beauty | 124 |
| The beast | 125 |
| All that nature | 127 |
| Some steps | 128 |
| Songs of a dictator | |
|     1: He woos his mistress | 129 |
|     2: He regrets his youth | 130 |
|     3: His philosophy | 132 |
| Poems for Television | 133 |
| A Requiem | |
|     Introit | 137 |
|     Dies Irae | 140 |
|     Offertory | 144 |
|     Communion | 149 |
| For Ben | 151 |
| Notes | 152 |
| What the Glove Said | 158 |
| Bird | 159 |
| Prologue | 160 |
| Untitled | 161 |

| | |
|---|---|
| Cuneiforms | 163 |
| Ars Poetica | 165 |
| Nights I-V | 167 |
| Aubade | 172 |
| Divinations 1-12 | 173 |
| Nude with mirror | 187 |
| Yet | 188 |
| Tracing the damage | 190 |
| Afterwards | 193 |
| They do not arrive in time | 194 |
| In a restaurant | 195 |
| On the Death of God | 196 |
| Enduring freedom | 198 |
| La Belle Dame | 201 |
| Rising from Aquifers | 202 |
| Owl Songs I-III | 206 |
| Medea | 217 |
| I will write | 218 |
| Flames | 219 |
| A digression | 220 |
| This window | 222 |
| Saint | 223 |
| Witchcharm | 224 |
| Poem for Zoe | 226 |
| The wind | 227 |
| Money | 228 |
| Language | 229 |
| Where are the dark woods? | 230 |
| Mnemosyne I-X | 231 |
| Phrases | 241 |
| Suttee | 242 |
| From the West Gate Bridge | 244 |
| I like to think about my beloved | 245 |
| Once upon a time | 246 |
| The letters of the good mothers | 247 |

| | |
|---|---|
| Poetry on tv | 249 |
| Thoreau in Chernobyl | 251 |
| Persephone | 252 |
| In the hour of dogs | 254 |
| The virgin bride | 255 |
| Euterpe | 256 |
| Mayakovsky | 257 |
| Words | 258 |
| A History of Rain | 259 |
| To break a silence | 261 |
| Specula | |
|     Visions of the world's surface | 262 |
|     Of Margery of Kempe I | 264 |
|     Of Life's Mys(t)eries | 266 |
|     Of Margery of Kempe II | 268 |
|     The Unknown Language | 270 |
|     Of Margery of Kempe III | 271 |
|     Dance of the Seven Veils | 273 |
|     Of Margery of Kempe IV | 276 |
| The Kingdom | 277 |
| O my america | 279 |
| If in foregone times | 281 |
| There are breakages certainly | 282 |
| Why I Am Not A Scientist | 283 |
| Bees | 284 |
| Couplets | 285 |
| Alley | 289 |
| Schwittering | 290 |
| Theatre | 291 |
| Goodnight, sweet prince | 293 |
| Iseult | 294 |
| Possible Elegies | 296 |
| On lyric 1-11 | 303 |

Notes on the poems

# The poet has no identity

The poet has no identity. She is an electrical cloud she is a swarm of bees she is a kabuki scream she is a shadow on the blind the plates in a cupboard the roar of trucks on a freeway. She is the fiery neurone and the mark on a piece of paper. She speaks on the telephone into the ether. No one there. Maybe it is god. She writes her body with the tips of her fingers but it is no longer her body. The words are not her they belong to nobody. She writes to slough off her name. She speaks to become invisible. She desires to become what she is. When she wakes into her name it is falling asleep again. When she dreams she forgets. She is blind. She has the power of flight.

# Why I don't like being photographed

*For Nicholas Walton-Healey*

the true fact is that I am invisible
                        the light that bounces off my skin
      through the aperture of a lens is quite
                            a different phenomenon and is possibly
a spectre who will walk around
               inside the shape my name is supposed to be
                          ordering books on the murderousness of opera
                or secondhand Dior nighties
      or committing acts of production that wake me in terror at 2am
          or conversing with unsavoury strangers
in the corners of the internet
                        it is very confusing

like the invisible clouds that liquefy the tundra
                        the phantoms won't stop proliferating
     they keep sending me emails that I can't read
                no matter how hard I squint they
     are never about what they seem to be
success love happiness no one seems to know
                            how to escape into another dimension
                stuck on our mundane sofas watching that movie
     where the monster wriggles inside our very skins
          and in their mansions up on the hill the dead-eyed madmen
              whisper it out and feed it every morning
it all ends in explosions that's what it's for
          and then we export the virus to another planet
      as if there had been a time when once we were

more than data transmission in brutal economies
                      yet still we go on imagining
        rainbows and other physical objects
hovering beautifully in the vapour of our breaths


I am never quite sure who is thinking
        perhaps it is me or perhaps it is my photograph
    who maybe went fishing which I have never liked
                    and is admiring how the light
ripples its endless changes over the same river


    when I'm especially sad
            I like to read Viktor Shklovsky who was
the saddest critic of all and who always began
                his books with a description of a landscape
        those were optimistic days
    he said the nightingale doesn't know
        that it has been refuted
                he said a riddle always has two answers
    one is literal and wrong and the other
renews meaning by rearranging things
    I wonder if there are still crows in Yalta
            one day I would like to buy him coffee
    and we could converse in cyrillics about fairytales
    and how art has its own laws
and how a poem is a riddle of sorts and not like a photograph
    which may be another kind of riddle
                  but dissimilar
      of course

# Ode

We were woken too early, before the moths had died in the streets,
when buds had barely hardened in the frost, when stars are hurtful
and famished. They took us through gardens and past the halls
where once we had lingered, past the houses and doused markets.
Our footsteps echoed back like iron. Of course we were frightened,
that was a given, of course we remembered photographs we had studied
that then had nothing to do with us. The empty light of morning
made anything seem possible, even freedom, even God. We stumbled
on familiar roads, and everything turned away from us,
lamp-posts, windows, signs. They weren't ours any longer. Even the air
greeted us differently, pinching our skin to wake us from its dreams.

\*

Words of course were beyond us. They were what killed us
to begin with. They were taken away from the mouths that loved them
and given to men who worked their sorceries in distant cities,
who said that difficult things were simple now and that simple things
no longer existed. It was hard to find our way, we understood
the tender magic of hands, we knew the magic of things not spoken,
but this was a trick we couldn't grasp. It lifted the world in a clump of glass
and when everything came back down the streets had vanished.
In their places were shoes and clotting puddles and sparking wires
and holes and bricks and other things that words have no words for
and that silence swelling the noise until you can't hear anything at all.

\*

It's said that the dead don't dream, but I dream of flowers.
I could dream so many flowers – lilies like golden snow on water,
hyacinths the colours of summer evenings or those amaranths they call
love-lies-bleeding. I dream of none of those. I dream instead
of wind-blown roses that grew in our shabby yard, of daisies
glimpsed through the kitchen window, of marigolds that glowed
through nets of weed. But most of all, I dream of red anemones
that never grew in my garden. They rise on slender stalks,
their seven-petalled heads bobbing and weaving in the wind.
Wind-flowers, Pliny called them, because they open only in the wind,
and the wind scatters their petals over every waste in the world.

# Poetry you never lied to me

So where do you land when your eyes are finally working
so well you can barely see instead you look
inside out as the worms in your brain work through
to the page like economists adding up zeroes
you live in this world it opens its arms it's exactly
what you feared those dreams when you can't stop
the tortured boy printed on your retina the hole
in his cheek the slashed arms bloodless now the
cigarette burns how did they yes they did they always do
the big stupid money fracking the laws of mercy
all the connections clear and obscene like being haunted
by lino in kitchens that the years have demolished
into visions of mothers in aprons with lacquered hair
squawking of migraines or bending over shining ovens
for their hygienic children and executive husbands
you staggered in toxic heels and vomited blood
it was was gentler than madness your sister's terror
that slashed her to ribbons her visions of Lear her naked pain
poetry you never saved me but you were a rail of words
that promised a kind of redemption you knew it was fake
but out of the distance stepped those ample summers
real as the camellias that opened outside your window
red as your fingers red as your newborn babies beautiful vaginas
speaking the possible here in this same world
where chemical hells scour the skin from children
o poetry who stepped down and clapped her manacles
speaking her sentences knowing the judgement is life
her fluid chains her solitary rooms her knives of ice and blood
opening inside you like forgiveness you think of your sisters

and you laid out in columns neat and shy and obedient
polishing skirtings weeding the roses waiting for the devil to visit
and run his finger along the shelves and find us wanting
but he can go to hell him and his little brothers
all those feminine lessons I flung on the fire of my ego
refusing death although I invited him in with every word
every cigarette every failure poetry you never lied to me

# Beasts

The beasts are retreating. They are sliding
into the dusk, into the supple light of vanishing trees,
into the glue of dreams. All their strangeness
wavers behind wire, between the four sides of a screen,
odourless and deathless. The beasts stare out of
bleached pages, enclosed at last, and the zoos
are silent, except when parrots and keepers
conduct their weird orchestrations.
Panic flicks in those slotted eyes but the sadness
is only ours. Police hunt corpses in rubbish dumps,
a pregnant mother and child. Beneath the surface,
submarine cries burst the ears of whales.
Coral is leached to stone by the stripped sunlight
and houses crouch by the shore, awaiting the wave
prophets see in the distance. In forests
that glow at night, there are boars and wolves
whose futures mutate daily. There is much that is unknown
as always and even more that now will never
be understood. The cedar forests of Lebanon
are tinder dry and bears starve on the wet tundra.
In the depths of night there may be a phone call
we dare not answer or a cry in the street
which makes the hair rise on the back of our necks.
They will not come back, something is happening
at the edge of our eyes, behind the reflections,
and billboards shout in the silence, delivering words
that in a more innocent age we thought were ours.

# Quickening

*quick en, v.t. & i. Give or restore natural or spiritual life or vigour to, animate, rouse, inspire, kindle, whence ~ing a.; receive, come to, life (of woman or embryo)*
- The Shorter Oxford Dictionary

## I  Family Notes

### 1

at first I was afraid
howling my weird losses in a cot
this I remember clearly

also the red of veldt fires
boiling the road with shadows
my first suspicion of an alien land

it is hard to trace these things:
where a barrenness starts,
a dry raw thing unnoticed in the valleys

and later, looking down from a hill,
the traveller flinches in strange recognition
having always suspected it was there

**2**

water
it was safe in baths
but what was this    looking down from a ship
of fatly painted iron in Durban harbour
a surface full of glassy lips
and underneath it shifting fathoms of red
my father said
jellyfish    and the small tug loosed me
four years old into my first ocean


when I was five or six
I nearly jumped
the bridge was narrow steel and swayed in the high air
I wanted to surprise its chains
and the mean-windowed prim-roofed Cornish houses
shut hard against the harbour's green snake eye


Australia was practical and taught me swimming
O the unnatural blue hiccup    the blue smart of baths
a boy with sunshocked hair
taught me nature's laws:
dive in the deep end he said and you can't go wrong
because everything floats
I jumped so heavy with faith I had to be rescued

and so learnt to respect from shores
the eye without lids and the mouthless tongue which has no complexion
except the colours it steals from above and beneath
and within the breathless glitter of imagined fish
but the sea moved in my dreams
those prickling dreams forgotten
in the numbing light of an alien dawn

**3**

Unhappiness is easier to live with
than you think.
You walk around with it like a limp
compensating   compensating   compensating

I knew God had abandoned us
in this shallow land.
I knew the ash-dry grass was a joke
mocking our lush memories of green.

The fleshy flowers of a gentle spring
and cultured woods
haunted our hedged dreams.
Our heads lay in the starlight on bony hills

in harsh summers when the heat crushed
all water from the air
and the dam drew back a poverty of gasping reeds
and snakes came to sip from the hose.

**4**

      what is this phrase
uncurling itself

      the trees are silent
and winnow the sky
         with gnarled hands

      the birds sing
but their song
         only deepens the silence

## II  Love Poems

**1**

she hides in the distracting veils
of midnight silences


this is her bed and this her lover
turning now like oil at her side
this is the space she counts inside herself
one   two   this white silence


she tastes it privately
like rare soft delicious fruit
praying that her lover will not speak

2

my usual magnificent morning.
first it was sunny
and now it threatens to rain
and all the nappies
will have to be dried inside.


I have simply shuffled things around
so they look better.
the same amount of mess
squats in the corners.
Tomorrow it will reveal its true nature.


meanwhile I have preserved
my invisible vows
and have spoken to no one
except the telephone
a jealous cat and my baby.


afterwards perhaps I will sleep
if my other task fails me.

**3**

I watch the moon
through a small window
bloating and shrinking

always the night devours me
down to a nameless
unlucky hunger

wherever you go
with your mean love
I will follow you

a shriek in your brain
a claw in your testes
a manacle on your tongue

**4**

love never stopped a bullet
or stayed the raping hand
of a damaged world
but it is the only way
to remain undefeated

I know your body solid
under my palm
I know the gates of your skin
the ways of your mouth
all these I tell as endlessly
as the renewing day

but in my dreams
how easily devoured:
we crouch small and white
under an ominous sky
all we have for shelter
a seed of light in our hands

**5**

loneliness.
it binds me to itself like a lake
eating my face with ripples.
shadows crawl in its thick depths.
I can guess their shapes although I lack
a saint's disinterested equanimity
which tweezes parasites from stinking sores
forgiving them their nature.
I can guess what they are:
they are armoured and vicious things
their mouths are ugly with all the habits of greed.
if I hook them out with steely fingers
they will be small and limp and pallid
disgusting as excuses.
I recognise them all. I do not want to.
tonight I can't be passionless and distant.
I want a room of faces blurred with chat
drinking comfortably from shallow glasses.
I find an acid mirror which dissolves me
to the bitter arch of bone.

## III  Howl

**1**

my lover is not here
to touch the child
rolling in my womb


o unbearable innocent
how will you smile
in this hive of lies

**2**

Hell is never private by design
there's always some damned neighbour peering in
or dogs barking insanely at the disturbance
at the very least the greedy roar of traffic
going somewhere else

it happens so quickly you don't know
what sins you're being punished for
or how long eternity is

not to mention the humiliations
flames wreak on flesh:
the bubbling eyes
the loss of every sense except pain

**3**

Love is the generous blood crushed from pleasure
the blood of our suffering
it is the hinge between the heart and the world
it evades the will's machinery but there is nothing subtle about love
it is the heart singing to itself, I love you


and those not loved enough
who carry their nervous hearts like chilled glass
who delicately place them on a ledger, saying this is the price
who open their wounds to the wounded sadist
who mouth love's legislation but not its confusion
who wash out the filth of love with blinding astringents
who smell only decay in love's spiced gardens
who disembowel love, crying treachery
how will they be healed
in the arms of love?


in their brutal ghettos the children gather
with incised faces:
their eyes are stained, their souls are damaged out of them
they claw the city's acid dugs
they are coming for us, craftily in our heads
they will carve their emptiness
inside us

**IV  Domestic Art**


pain grabbed me cruelly and tossed me
into the violent land of my body.
all around were ravines and crags
and the freefall of exhaustion.
the only way out was through. at the end
you split out of me like a ripe seed
and opened your unused eyes on my sweating skin


\*


neither maid nor matchless
neither still nor blest
I woke with knowledge in my womb
and fear within my breast


the day was five hours old
when Joshua wriggled out
to see what all the dim reports
of noise were all about


he is a knot of needs
my ends are all astray
and the hours are short and fat
with Joshua in my day

somewhere a poem is invented
        for a sleeping child it has
a greek simplicity the whitest
        sheets to signify
the unwritten the poem
may contain a flute or a slow
        drum but no
sharp instruments even though
the crescents pencilled in
by sleep and the breath are
        easily erasable the poem
bruises secretly the deepest
        muscles of pleasure

\*

rise into me like new cake
bunched and sorry you loud snout
bursting your sheaf of blind
legs you lust of fists writing
all over me squiggles and
drizzles of must o my
juicy suckling out of the
oven and perfectly
crusted all over with smiles

\*

There's nothing much surprising about washing nappies
except that shit is such strange colours, a sloppy spectrum of yellow.
You become inured to it, like standing in cowpats for warmth
on frost mornings or mucking out stables with your hands.
However, it's no accident that Jesus
washed the feet of his disciples.
Folding the laundered cloths, you may find
an unsettling capacity for grace.

*

a ball of thumbs
eyeing the suckable

winks and smiles
and colours like food

snarling my innards
I shall not sleep

or I'll wake empty
in skinless dark

*

you open and shut like wavelidded oceans you squall your greed you offer
        your treasures
humbly I unravel your absolute languages

you sprang from love like a new god unstable and charged as weather
a tyrant of toilsome needs I bend low and serve you
now I feel my funeral its alleluias
arching under my flat pulse
holding your hard skull a helpless worship utterly dependent utterly separate

always under the patches and scuffs the indomitable cell the living pattern of
        you

my soul is elastic my senses billow like nets to draw in your voices
your sleep lipping my sleep my sunflower skin beaming to you
more than the shock of reflection rather a blaze
in a mansion of unknown rooms and my chilled
hunger welcomed in and generously feasted at a table always my own

# Emily Bronte

these windy slopes are shorn
of the things which make life comfortable:
broad trees, broken bread, the swell

and supple curve of a lover's back.
I sit here by my window, catch
the rough, sweet scent of heather in my nostrils

and write of death and love entwined
like adders together. The poetry
lies wild in my veins, the poetry

of granite skies stabbed by rocky outcrops,
the giving spring of turf, the taste
of solitude like aloes on my tongue,

the bare unchanging moors, which take
my sisters and myself with mute indifference
and conquer under soil all our passion.

# The Elwood Organic Fruit and Vegetable Shop

I will go walking in Elwood with my mind as smooth as a marrow
winking at the unruffled sky throwing its light down for free
letting the gardens exude their well-groomed scents and thinking everything
        good
to the Elwood Organic Fruit and Vegetable Shop:
for the counter is democratically in the centre and everyone smiles
for people go on with the civil business of buying and selling under the hand
        written notices
for bawling children are solaced with grapes and handled to leave no bruises
for the mangoes are soft yellow thighs and the strawberries are klaxons of
        sweetness
for the mignonette purses its frilly lips and snowpeas pout their discreet
        bellies and the melons hug their quirky shapes under their
        marvellous rinds
for onions ringing their coppery globes and o the silver shallots and the hairy
        trumpets of leeks
for the cabbages folding crisp linens and the broccolis blooming in purple
        tulles and the dense green skirts of lettuces
for peaches like breasts of angels and passionfruits hard and dark and
        bursting with seed in your palm
for the dull gold flesh of pontiacs and knotty umbers of yams and new
        potatoes like the heels of babies
for the tubs of sweet william and heart-lifting freesias and orchids damp and
        beautiful as clitoral kisses
for poignant basil and maiden-haired fennel and prim blue-lipped rosemary
        and o! irrepressible mint!
how they nestle up the vegetables, promising them the fragrance of their
        ardour!
the marriages which await them! the lips that moisten to meet them! glorious
        speech of the earth!

# Amplitudes

**1**

Never enough but always that desire which returns
And it always does return, although the stars are not propitious
They say for example today that I will be offered more opportunities than I
    can accept
And I take that to mean the kisses which will not fit on my skin
Which has grown private overnight and wishes to hide its shames
        Having been too much looked on lately and too much taken for sale
Nevertheless I will not write the lines which are so requested
        I will not stroke the coiffures of the well-satisfied
Who sit there with their hungry eyes demanding analgesic recognitions and
    a sly laugh
Who cultivate their certainties and never stumble over their shrunken
    ambitions
It is not for me to invoke the compassions of their insomnias nor to debate
    their infidelities and mortgages
Their dreams are dreams of triumph and their nightmares tidied away and
    put out every Monday for collection
And their losses are hidden for failure is feminine like an unfashionable
    rhyme

## 2

Survival is so much more than the food you prepare for the table
It is of course the potatoes but also the chives you flavour them with and the
      candles glowing above the floral feast
           And the libations offered up in the spillages of the soul
It is the gasp of undulled want that peeps out unbidden
As if a goddess beckoned from the jacaranda and vanished, leaving the
      mundane world pregnant with her radiance
As if remnants of her absence glinted through the tiny hairs on a loved arm

**3**

Captains of Industry! I salute your fidelity to the narrowness of your desire!
For my desires are narrower still and how much more sublime!
In my indolence I may encompass entire globes of want!
I have banked invisible notes against the wintry soul in my untraceable
        black economies!
I am sensible as a angel, being the mouth of a fabulous excess!
                My thrift is beyond measure!


O my sad Captains, when at last you drain the lees of your fearfulness
When at last the time you worshipped opens its stony palms and demands
        payment
When you discover that cold ache no theory will propitiate
Perhaps you will think of me and my ascetic impracticalities!
Perhaps then you will deign to envy me my glittering fountain, which
        gushes its impossible wealth of pain!


I am alive!
        And only death can stop me.
                        (And even that's not certain)

## 4

Was it me at the well
Me who caused much whispering because I would not take my second cousin
        for a husband although he was rich and old
Because he had a wart on his nose and fat wet hands
                And because I had a lover I would talk about to no one
But my lover married a woman with many fields and goats and I hit the walls
        with my bloody fists
And then I went out and screamed in the grass where we had laid down
Where he had held the rose of me in his trembling mouth


And I told no one


Now my knuckles are scarred and my beauty is gone and forgotten
        But still the women whisper about me
                And I walk to the well alone


And the man said, buy me a drink
I turned and laughed in his face and said, what, you ask me? and who the
        fuck are you?
He leant over the bar his beaten face all crossgrained under the coloured
        lights and he said:
I hold within me such unquenchable thirsts that you will die thinking of how
        you refused them
And it will be you begging me for the ineluctable water
Which burns your throat as if it were acid and which you may drink without
        stint

Until it flowers inside the unknowing core of yourself
        Pure innocent pain such as you haven't known
                Since the instant of your birth
Which of course you can't remember
                        So I bought him a drink

And he said...

5

You will only want me when your life no longer makes any sense to you
     And I will offer you no consolation
Although of course my hands will be purple with all the grapes I have eaten
And my arms will smell of the children I have held and my breasts will be
  starred with spargosis
And twined in my hair the bays and the ivies although I give them no heed
I have always stood here naked, waiting your coming, and I will show you no
  pity
            That is a promise


I can only say, of course! It was always like that! How is it that you didn't
  know?
And now in this terrible clarity you will put on everything that is human
Your skin that you left behind you, while you were thinking that you were
  God
And all your desire lay within the span of your will!


Did you think your muse was gentle, dipping her sandalled foot in a lapping
  brook?
You were blind if you did not see how she turned everything to stone
Behind her eyes were fountains of lava
      Perhaps you stopped your ears saying such things
  Are not the intelligences of civilisation
But poetry is barbaric, the nursery chant of the dispossessed
    Crude and sad and throbbing
      Flesh gleams basely through its brilliant baubles
  And from its eyes the beams of darkness visible

                             Cast sullen ruminations
             Virgil that eager lackey of Empire
                       But still Dido howls in her pyre -
      And think how Athena bribed the nightmaires
                                  Bathing the law in their bloody logic
Love hacked into its sexes
                    Breeding hate


           Since Tiamat's dismembered corpse was scattered in swampy Ur
When her intestines were spread over the sky like a terrible raincloud
                 And her cunt became the cave
                    A decent man dares not enter
The poet is homeless and bitterly
                       Sings her want in the face of the primal crime
Which opened its eyes on that first watery horizon
            And since then all has been war
                       Even the smallest glasshouse


For poverty might be all we know of freedom
                                 Slaves know love solves nothing
But nevertheless sing of love
                       Scrubbed of its illusions
                How it lies on the bed its scrotum all anyhow
In the lovely limb-tossed languor of itself
                       Its breath soured with intoxicants and the folds
            Of its skin slantwised into shadow

Knowing there is nothing else apart from death
                        Purchasing a little life with the waters of your tongue
Having nothing else to heave against the weariness of the labours
        Which cripple your hands and clot your beating veins
              A little love and a little wine
      Sipped on a bench in the shadow cast by a wall
Might sometimes be enough
              And sometimes not
                          Sometimes not at all

**6**

For that it is noble to die of love
        Is a wisdom only those who are poor
                Can chew down to the core

# 7

Is it true that you can see through words as if they were luminous fish
                All the way to Babylon?
Is it true that language is the breathing azure tide
          Lifting its other hem on the shores of myrtle haunted Knossos?
How old are these skins we know ourselves by? Are they bright as the plastic
      raincoats
You buy for a single shower and throw out for landfill?
                  Why does the crumbling stone reveal my daughter's profile
      Before the Temple's portal?
                        And yet she runs out freshly in her muddy adidas
   With a long string of coloured beads pinned into her hair
And the aromas of a cheap perfume, lily of the valley or watermelon,
      sweeten the air around her

**8**

There are always many to praise war
                                              Even their condemnations praise it
They become hard and full like cartoon heroes, their chests lumpy with
      indignation
Right is with them and so it ever shall be world without end
                  And how they love their voices rising up to the heavens
How they love the radium polish of their hardened missiles, which so
      neatly resolve all equations
Only Me! they cry O the beautiful sound of Me! And O you Others you Them
They who do not exist except in their obliterations
                                  They whose eyes only exist for the Me
Which rises bright as a thousand suns over an edgeless saltpan
          A blank white glare
                                Hearing no answers
Because there are no answers


What has this to do with me?
                 Everything of course. It has little to do with I
                          Crouching in my margins mumbling selves
I am I was not I will not be I am
                          Sheer breath
      Breathed into the cave of another's mouth


But nevertheless I do not exculpate *them*
                I refuse their borders as the wind refuses
            Wishing to abide
                  In all my complicities

We have silenced the frogs of Ecuador and the dew-heavy clouds of
        Amazon have vanished because of us
In the corals of Barbados and Whitsun the polyps are bleached to calcium
Whales keen in the breeding grounds and deer no longer rut in the Tyrolean
        hills
Even the krill of Antarctica know something is wrong
          And my children will never walk between shaggy trees in a primal
            eucalypt forest
                The unknown has been parcelled out for sale
And its waves and velocities, its cascading joys and terrors, its intimate
      enmities, its purrs and chirrupings and scales, its fibrous
      flagellant sisterhoods, its intricate immensities
Are become a single dying howl
            Beyond the range of our hearing

**9**

*Ego Borago gaudia semper ago*

        I borage bring alwaies courage
    Quoth the wise man among his simples
      His garden an Empire


     Indian Swallow Wort
Which groweth in that part of Virginia, or Norembega, where our English
   men dwelled (intending there to erect a certain colony):
The Floure of the Sun, or the Marigold of Peru, which grow of
   themselves without setting or seeding
Also calld Corona Solis or Sol Indianus, others Chrysanthemum Peruvianum
   or the Golden Floure of Peru:
Tabaco, or Henbane of Peru, which cleeres the sight and taketh away the
   spots and webs thereof, being anointed with the juyce bloud-warme:
     Apples of Love
       That even in the hottest time of Summer
          Contain a great coldnesse
Which I leave to every man's censure


Indigenous herbs of wood and hedge of course in abundance
   Windfloures Selfheale Madder Teasels and the Pennie Royalle
    But unknown to Pliny for example
        The sweatbees of Gondwanaland
     And the ghost mists of jungle highlands
The desert's scarlet pea or a particular
     Aqueous blue of saltbush
   Which might never acclimatise themselves
       To the King's Gardens

**10**

And beside the mark of Hammurabi the songchants to fretful babies
                Next to the cloth of gold the rotted cottons
Beside a hero's cauldron this shattered clay impregnated with oils of leaf and
        nut and grain
Beside the broken weapon the nascent glance of a lover
                        The looms and hands and lips all perished
The worlds they loved and suffered vanished like waves
                              And as surely repeated
Again and again the infinite various curves of speaking lips
        Erased in the hypnotic clash of weapons


And if it is said this is but sentimental trivia
                        I shall claim for myself the steeliest realism
For nothing human survives but for these things
        And I will refuse the apocalypse
                Which man has dredged out of his loneliness
                        Voting himself the powers of a god


And what of the silenced million millions?
        Those tossed onto history's dump and bulldozed into geology
How to think of them, so nonsensically dissolved into numbers
For we are them pressing up against the glass of ourselves
                            And they are not us as nobody is ever me
And despite this the old murders continue in the untended lots of our
        disregard
Because the landlord must have his exquisite collections of MiGs
Because the ash clouds of Sumatra are more profitable than orangutans

Because of the beautiful vacant gaze of television
Because the acid blue lakes of Roumania make the Mafia happy
Because the price of amber has fallen through invisible floors
Because divine discontent is but the perfect expression of a growing
        economy
Because money swirls through the stratosphere
               A virus mutating through billions of transactions intangibly
                    as a cloud of hydrocarbons
Going from nowhere to nowhere
               And almost everyone is sick with it
                            And the rest are mad


               And given that despair is no answer
                      And that defiance makes no difference
And that silence is a death and saying another kind of dying
       And in any case the word was corrupt from the very beginning


Even with the blood on my hands
                         And my mouth toxic with contrition

## 11

And while pondering defiance and the melodrama of gestures
And words which sit demurely on a white page written over for vanity
Or if not vainly then out of impotence and despair
                                        Which amounts to the same thing
        A cheque might arrive tomorrow or the next day
                                               Or might not
I am consequently thinking of what might pay for my dinner
            Thereby measuring sincerity by lack
                    Since I have nothing to fall back on
                                Not being a *sensible person*
As that film director said so sadly on the phone once from Los Angeles
Quite correctly since the vacant lures of Hollywood were less profitable than
      a poem
                                And so it has certainly proved so far
Although like Brecht we write dollar signs in our diaries
            Enamoured like all the unelect by that magnificent mirage


                                    Unfortunately eating is necessary
And despite many contemporary innovations exploring the quotidian
        materiality of language
                Nobody but silverfish can eat poems
Which is of course sufficient reason not to write them
                          Except as a hobby for the creatively inclined
But I have always been too literal minded
          I thought of the stony mouth of Kassandra
I took Rilke at his word
                And have always understood capability as negative

The stars today said I would receive a small gift
                              But the postman's bag was empty
Perhaps an angel blazed in the doorway while I was otherwise occupied
      In fact my son kissed me many times on my face
                    And told me that he loved me

## 12

Am I the only person left who reads poetry on the train
                    I have sometimes wondered
Trace of an age which never existed
          Not even in the minds of those who thumbed soft yellowing pages
                  Adumbrating absolute laws of self, beautiful Godhead
                  emanations
                                    *Sum quia sum*
The manly spirit idling by a glorious stream of knowing and being
          Dazzled by the mind's dynamic abstractions
                            While his child dies of smallpox
                  Beyond letterless rivers of ice

For poetry is a pitiless terrain
                    No artist puzzles over the deathcamps

The logical brain of a predator sending its sonar over the rippled depths
The precise brutal design of a jaw
The ear scanning for furtive scuffles under a crust of snow
The bullet fall of a gannet to the bruising sea surface
                                Are the inadmissable graces of art

Who hasn't felt the cold seduction of beauty?
              Warping the real into a dead ideal
                              We've nearly got there

    And a cold inferno it is indeed
        Teeming with isolate souls
      Screaming through the vibrating silence of earless matter

**13**

*People will behave like that on Judgement Day*
        *Sipping honey from poisonous flowers*
*Worshipping the dying sun as the giver of life*
        *Kissing the dying earth as the mother of fruitfulness*


        Meanwhile despair's violent children
Raise their empty hands to the sky and cry Death, seeing
    A cleansed world unfold before their eyes
        And mark the designated doors
            With crosses of black angels


    O how seductive that single note
We'll scrape the world back and start again properly
        And how many starts have started
Since the first homicide breathed that pure denial out of his green nostrils
        The same lie in a new suit
      Wakes beneath a dream of absolute pillars

## 14

And how to understand these infinite networks
Outside for example looking at the stars like my million forebears and with
    the same irreducible awe
Although I understand the light on my retina as the intrusion of an
    unimaginable past into my unimaginable present
From stars long dead or even now flaring into desuetude
Collapsing upon their unsustainable masses or expanding in a billowing
    coruscating tide
Vast energies we seek to domesticate with equations
Devising ever more complex maps to extend our optics only to gaze at them
    with animal eyes
Themselves admitting collisions of light to fire the webby neurones
Which we map also with that same propertied delight
                          Looking ever inward to endlessly receding galaxies
Dividing into electrons neutrons photons protons gravitons those quantum
    gods vibrating through incomprehensible ecstasies
Until they too collapse in contradiction and reveal that the universe itself is
    impossible
Because the recurring answer is eternity
                          Meaning that the question is wrong


And if I can't find myself among the eleven dimensions
Which are immeasurably more remote than Dante's Florence or the
    domestic life of Athens
                It proves nothing
Not even if God exists

         Which is also the wrong question
     I however am quite certain that I exist
  I am merely uncertain


Being however human I must make some things matter
            For my own convenience
And against the dazzling cosmogony of significance place my own
   insignificant loves
      As each of us, humbly in our vulnerable flesh
        Faces the vast blankness of death

**15**

Mind is invisible and therefore does not exist
        Requiring a costume to be audible
                Knowing not seeming

As I am invisible in my dressing gown, checking the mailbox in the morning
                For missives on my personal economic disaster
Nevertheless mind sings
        Strangely
                    Beyond the impediments of speech
Accidents of chromosomes and class
                Becoming whatever
Is not received into histories

    Mind is invisible and therefore exists
        Beyond sclerosing boundaries and finds
Its way into words
        Sometimes
                And sometimes music
May remember itself under the noise
        Undoing the brutalities, may amuse
            Freely to itself
                May find
Its gentleness, being invisible, how easily it may not
    Be
        And so be
            Seeming nothing

# Poem for John

You ask for a poem
and I say
I have no poem

here the sky
which embraces both of us
in this single world
is blue
and I read
that birds sing
between the bombs
in Iraq

no balance
no consolation
and no answer
as the angel of history
turns its vengeful face
towards us all

you are right

we need poems
as we need bread
we hunger for that blue
human milk
to nourish our largeness
to minister our pain
and our love

here is your poem

# Ode to Walt Whitman

Did you see me Walt Whitman beside my meagre river where I walk at
      sunset with my children
Who whinge and buffet my arms and will not be led in any direction
Marching with my sight closed to the rain and skittering seagulls while my
      children shouted look!
As the incandescent leaves shouted look! individual and numberless under
      the sodium light
Although I hurried on nagging and impatient:
Did you hear the haul of the empty trains into the vanishing twilight
Turning my face like a mint coin hope stamped on my mouth
To a night ambiguous with satellites
Hearing in my secret heart the radio noise of murders half a suburb away
Which all the loud news fails to report -
Walt Whitman there are evenings when love withers inside me
The beat you thrummed with your syllabled fingers those joyous rebellious
      prosodies:
Did you see the muscles of your teeming world
Smashing the earth unstringing the massive harp of the sky
When you sang of your body returning alert as grass
Or thrust out the spokes of your sight into the great unchanging wheels
      the miraculous sun and the tumultuous impersonal sea -
Walt Whitman the gods are tarnished now the cities mourn their dead
      no longer
Children roast in the fires of this terrible century
And no love is enough no elegy sufficient:
And yet I imagine you gentle imperfect generous man I would like to
      talk to you
Perhaps you sit already at my shoulder whispering that nothing changes
That sunset is enough for its brilliance decay enough for its iridescence

Old faker with your wise beard your lustful piety:
And truly what is my faith
Except a stubborn voice
Casting out its shining length to where I walk alone
Sick and afraid and unable to accept defeat
Singing as I was born to

# All Souls Day

The dead have come to visit.
I don't know who they are.
They mark the glittering streets
With footsteps of rain.
The last leaves of autumn
Are their lost hands. I
Can almost hear their voices,

A rumour of wind and water.
My chest shakes like a window.
I have nothing to give them.
When I show them my hands
They turn away, disappointed.
Their eyes see through walls
To irrevocable horizons. I

Do not know their names.
Their breath beats in my arteries
Like ash, like earth, like rain
Which will never stop falling.
Their injuries taint my mouth
With a taste like blood. I
Breathe their sour bones.

I do not know what they want.
They seep into every cell
The purities of their lack.
Knowledge crumbles against them
And pours into a vast river
Where I am nameless.
The dead have come to visit

Hungry as birds in winter,
Enclosed by mortal grief
As light encloses a gesture
In darkness. I do not know
If it releases them.
Only the living are sad.
*Dona eis requiem.*

# A flower

*IM Jeremy Rasmussen*

I don't want a gravestone.
I would rather scent the night
with spores of wild grass.
If others wish to remember me,
they might walk out under a full moon
and breathe me in with the plain air.
It would be fitting and it would please me.
But the dead are beyond pleasing
and the living require something solid
enough to bear the heaviness of flowers
which smell of the desire to touch
what can't be touched again.

# Billie Holiday

and did it frighten you
that stench in the dark heart of the flower
you pinned behind your ear


and did your skull eat out through your beauty
every time they pressed their faces in you
seeing in your drowning face how their flesh collapsed inside you
and how the pure note hardened like a child
and wouldn't give in you
even after everything was given

# Lindy

there were others   there were always others
dogs running in the hungry twilight
she was alone only at the crisis
when she screamed the world bent its greedy ear
when she smiled photographers came to listen
her face hooded itself and slept
in a chrysalis of stone

the icons of her dreams scattered in the desert
slowly they gathered them   dog's tooth   torn cloth
and labelled them with the ardour of converts
she reassembled her voices in the silence
the crow sat in her larynx telling the same truth always
the oracle broke and bled   the people turned away, debating
fashioning another legend

# Chekhov in Sakhalin

**1**

in the bright of winter
they say the path of a drunkard
shines in solid air

a zigzag manshaped tunnel
that collapses
at the corpse

spring vomits up the mud
the earth dissolves beneath you
like a woman in tears

and fleas of course
a visible liveliness
in every man's bed

one cannot dismiss
the petty miseries

it is possible for a man
to freeze through
and still walk

a few vowels of pain
keep everything moving

a noble soul
is a death sentence

**2**

the astonishing child breaks the face
of a puddle

she has a stick and a bad case
of worms

scars harrow her back and I suspect
syphillis

her laughter frightens the ducks
off the bog

beautiful eyes that burn
my retina

like a child pitiless but harder
and chaste

as the kiss on her brother's brow
when she asks me

if his coughing will kill him
now or later

her indrawn breath of calculation
how

she shifts him on her hip and says
eat, baby

but she will never read or write
any of this

**3**

harsh liturgies of morning
love's hurt bell

again and again
a single cruel melody

she asked me, laughing
are there crows in Sakhalin?

comedies of the body
lodge in me like maggots

forgiveness is irrelevant
my jokes smell of blood

**4**

It is impossible to measure the tyranny of distance
from one end of a whip to the other
is a whole continent


the comparisons of agony
this woman lost her dog
this man left his fingers in the snow


strange, when there are so many ways of dying
in the ordinary scheme of things
a twitch of the sky


will thumb us shut
and if god hides in this emptiness
the lips of innumerable cruelties


split him open like a blown corpse
nudged by little waves on a houseless shore
all his work unfinished

# November burning

what is it that I cannot remember
if I was old if I was wise I am neither
my hands close on nothing my womb is tired
my fingers are scarred with old scrubbings
all day I stared out the window
and gathered the old griefs

the old gods walking in the garden
and the child holding a flower
in the painting on the wall of a chapel
where the afternoon sun is a memory already

ancient confusions
the blood that refuses the hunger that will not listen
I would like to know some answers
but can barely shape the questions out of fear
there are no new questions
only questions that have always gone unanswered
must I ask them
every night and every morning of my life
must I ask them although there are no answers
every night and every morning

in the difficult night of prayer
when the gods do not attend
in the washing away of afternoons
in each crumb of solitude given and wasted
in the tough bitter bread of love
that grazes your mouth and leaves you gasping

in the halfheard voices
and the cheek offered and withdrawn
the city's voluble inattention
the penances of ignorance and sobriety
perhaps the humble one ignites his presence
a balm of water on a fevered forehead
that evaporates before it is sensed

or perhaps the pure white that one dreams
past exhaustion in a crumpled bed
after all the interactions
that demanded one be other than you are
merely an erasure of pain

o you who were fragrant as Lebanon
the groves of your undoing
now pumped up irrevocable chimneys
the sky a burning glass
and the lands wasted

the child with a flower in the chapel
who was once a child bribed with sweetmeats
scratching lice
and the flower long dust
and the promises made and unmade and forgotten
living in the glance

how easy to lament
to stare with grief across the dying garden
it was always dying

never for my children or my children's children
will Adrasteia, Amalthea, Ida and Cynosura
bend cool studious brows in the college of the bee
the deep caves of water are poisoned
never will the spring

\*

did it travel the oceans from Olympus
heeled with the spite of the dead
is it socketed by ranks of heavy skulls
icythosaurus diplodocus tyrannosaurus rex
a schoolyard chant of bones mounting up
to the delicate mammalian intelligence
is it daubed with hair and ochre on the rock
near the rainy season water
and carved in relief in the tombs of kings
to gaze forever over a dry sea
the stare of a jewelled woman
the light windowed on her globed eye
measured by a bored painter
each shut of the lid and each dust mote
moist with millennia of blinkings
how far is a glance
as it flickers and rests and moves on

what is it that I can't remember
the door suddenly still in its movement
and afterwards crystalline with a light
that never shone there
as if a god had stepped in that common place
shared by mites and cockroaches and ants
and a mouse running its stink over the floor
as if a child long mute spoke a word
and its echo budded into flame
in the minds of those who heard suddenly humbled
by an unexpected

or weight of the lamb
on a burnt tongue
or the twisted tap
in a smoking garden
a single wing flapping
a lone dog howling
a bent nail

in the bleak Novembers
when the first winds roar from the northern deserts
bringing flame to tinder forests
and ash falls in the suburbs like soft black stars
where frail old women read their fortunes

ravens tilt outside shuttered houses
summoning a red moon
through the blasted twilight

humble wooden houses
up like a match
ash black and grey ash
in the black garden

and the door swinging on its hinges
in a late damp breeze
from an ocean far away
in the cold south

who died? who died?
and next door untouched
the wind seasonally capricious
and the stars unfavourable
Venus low and urgent in the west
yet fifty metres south
honeysuckle dips a curling tongue
into cool air

in such a November
I come to the same questions
in another place
a landscape of bloated corpses
walls crumbled to ruin
and no sign of rain

\*

she who touches the forehead of the virgin
child sleeping with her hands
closed beneath her cheek as if in prayer
to brush back a lock that has fallen
and moves on a slow breath

she may not perfectly
step between the chasms of illchoice
she may have betrayed herself
again and again
she may be foolish
and no longer hope for redemption

she may shiver with an awe
in a stained church where no one is waiting
she may know a wren is moulting
into the blue of his wedding
on the wasteland past the power station
where melancholy scrub bends down
before a salted wind that whips
the endless complaining of seagulls
into a troubled sky

she may know nothing

she is bitten with anger at the old curse
thickening about her throat
she has been silenced too often
her voice rang clear over the silent fields
and then her lids shot open to the choking
stain
on the sky
the choked
sky

she has spoken excellently modest and low
she has been gentle in the ungentle nights
she has bled on the sheets giving birth

she is forced to blame herself
there is no one else to blame

she should never have been silenced

*

o you
applefoot
eyewing
starfreckle
when did you vanish


o moth sprayed to its final agony
crumbling its wings
on a table


you were always
a mute star lost in
brash sodium


useless


the wires spat you out
the smart dollars laughed
in the bars


forget nothing


remember how you lifted the child
running for a train
strong as a god
in the sweet rain

# The page cannot be found

the page cannot be found
in the lemon tree or the magnolia

ants are searching everywhere
swallows wind their intricate clocks

the orb weaver swallows her web
as if she knows something

children examine their footsteps
with microscopes and pranks

but it seems the page has erased itself
as clouds draw up the syllables of rain

as the magpie's lovely carolling
dissolves inside the ear

# after Arseny Tarkovsky

My life is a book
I open with love
and eat with my eyes
but it isn't enough

The fruit on my table
is plain as a hand
that offers its light
but it isn't enough

My love is a scar
the shape of a wing
or the speech of the lost
but it isn't enough

My soul is a star
the night is a nail
my thought is a rope
but it isn't enough

# The Gift

leaning into a reflection
that my eyes do not register
as my belly dissolves as I
vanish into the space
your eyes devour I have

no place to be either
woken or alone I have
no name and my lips
are colder than imagining
when I sleep on the ice

of dreams it is a vapour
of fear that rises it is
a cold anaesthetic fume
rising like a goddess
her chilly feathers

glancing on my skin
like kisses I have forgotten
or gestures flinching between
one shadow and another
I am often afraid

# Coma

Eden was a cold place
inhabited by whispers.
God left early
and I took what I could
as a child eats
the poor food
on a shabby table.
How I hated
the mean words
that stamped me out
in monotone!
I stuttered
through the coma
of childhood.
Now the drab skins
are ripped open
and behind them
pulses a brutal
human eye.

\*

All the trinkets she handed down to me.

Opalescent terrors. A carved box full of delicate resentments. The garnet of betrayal.

Her envious eye. Her knife. Her tiny hands.

Hidden behind an emptied language, that swallowed girl.

What fable of redemption rattles through those paranoid phylacteries?

A faecal madness hunting through the gloom. All those blank daughters.

\*

she never cried she never
tumbled into that wet mouth she
drew such leachings of drought
over the paper sky that birds
perched gasping on branches she
found herself lipless turned
back to the bony night each star
pitiless the moon tugging
her down to blasted seas she
uttered stones the words curled up
in spiders of dust she felt
rain pulse against her skin but all
her dreaming could not think
itself past those horizons
of parched white the whiter
flame the sun whose voice
rose so white and burned

# Songs of a Quiet Woman

lurching delicate as a snow queen down this street of greys
unfocussed exactly enough to miss the businessmen
goggling at my stockings   deciding
(as I twitch primly into the tram seat   my handbag
nestled on my lap like a puppy)   deciding
this will be a day of minor survivals:
etching a bloody mouth in fluorescent mirrors
or idly lacquering a hand of claws:
small weapons for a small war

\*

there is one streetlight which always
blinks off whenever I walk near it
coming home late and secretarial
to the hint of cats and cooking -
silently inside me something flexes
something unsurprised

\*

men of course   lately they are kind to me
although an acid starting in my sweat
erodes me like an argument:
snatched by hesitation in a shop
eloquent and secret with the smell of him
I feel sureness swelling like a bruise
forcing blood into lips breathless and reverent
this pearl in the corruption of my belief

\*

(yes please no trouble thankyou mother
it's been a pleasure because I do not know
how to be angry or ugly mother -
granny addled with sherry under bombs
in Winchester never raised her voice
or said a word back to your father
no matter what woman or what insults:
her eighty year old skin is white and powdered
and now she pisses in the basin mother
and I know the proper way to lay tables)

\*

to other things I turn the eye of god.
the tv's gorgon eye has glazed me over
and nothing touches me at all:
not famine fire fear or revolution.
only a shellshocked child in Beirut
firmly stroked to stillness by a nun.
he stared at her with eyes as black as hunger.
I wept then for the simple magic of hands

\*

the routine of coffee    the complicity
of cigarettes and gossip
this gentle leaning over narrow tables
into the sly glass of recognition:
I know I am dishonest in my dress
(she says to me)    I know I am dishonest
but all I ever knew was how to lie

# Attempts at being

i

inexplicable fire

surges flame into flame its blue
whip trawling deeps of skin
for secret tongues lit
to nerveflash

throat after throat
        claws to its coronal

ii

brief spring tempests

a single drop
at twigtip
glanced by sun
to eyebright

muteness
breathing in

a kind of song
crude enough
for ears to see
clearly

**iii**

neither too far nor too within
nor too immense nor too intangible

grass that smells
of human damp
where lovers were

magnolia
      agitated by the thrust
  of a small bird

the globe trembling
through its gravid course

neurones quick with
such music
    as shakes out angels

# Beginning again

For example, the way that tree. There's a bird in it that sounds like a burglar alarm.

Were you really there, or someone else?

The bird, the tree. The light on a particular building, at noon, with the sky behind it. A stone pavement in the rain.

For example. How it hurts to say that word, my. Or mine. Or I.

You are walking along a pavement and close beside the pavement are cars, they seem to be travelling too fast. All they can see is walls, the walls of buildings, embankments, gardens. The road is wet. And it happens that you must cross this road.  There are too many cars, and it is wet, and it is becoming dark, and although you can see the other side of the road, you cannot cross. Yet all these people in all these cars are travelling fast, as if they can see through the walls to something else. A bicycle? A dog?

For example. The river. It is brown, it is narrow, it is green, its banks are stone, it is black, it is choked with weed, it is wide, a stone bridge curves over it, or a single tarmac path fenced with cyclone wire, glistening in the moonlight. No matter, there is a river. It is a river made of water, like all other rivers. It runs towards the sea.

When you place your elbows on the bridge, you look into the water.

The light on the water. Some bounces back to your eyes, some breaks itself on the surfaces of waves. Some pierces the surface and sends brown shafts down into the body of the river. You look at the light.

The light is a different colour. You are used to the light shifting from morning to night. You are used to the yellow of the sunlight on the wall in the evening and the wide white light of morning. You know how the shadow falls from a pencil. But this light is a different colour. It is one of the colours of water, as if the air was made of water.

It might begin like that.

# Pause

Within the undivided moments
A train stops on a bridge
A woman's finger touches the rim of a man's mouth
A child hides in his secret place and names his collection of stones
A general tells his soldiers that justice is not possible

Within the undivided moments
A woman decides to speak the lie she has always told before
A man decides to publish the lie he has always published before
A lie becomes a truth and then a history
A student turns off the desk light beside a darkening window

Within the undivided moments
A baby tastes an orange for the first time
A soldier stamps on the hands of a little boy
A man loses his way in the endless garden

Within the undivided moments
A twig falls in an empty pathway
A moth rests in a margin of light beside the darkening window
A beetle pauses and turns at the edge of a puddle of blood
And above the vanishing lovers
Magnificent lords of cloud reveal again
Beauty that no one can see

# Leaves

each leaf is a tree which makes
everything more difficult every second
expanding like a breath in directions
it didn't anticipate, as if a face beckons
behind its shadow: I did not understand
how the sea folded like that in slow
complex darknesses under this huge moon
motionlessly roiling: and my hands
were leaves then suddenly no longer
pursuing anything and the blood sang
in my eyes, stilled leaves of light
flaming each into trees, the endlessly
rippled out ripples

the skin on my hands
grows older and life is more sad
than I could possibly imagine
when youth simply showed me
despairs. What multiplies there
under your face? o show me
your harmed skin, show me the white
unblemished fears, we are not as solitary
as all that, give me the scalpel which
severs us, surely now, even in
this corrupted air

                my daughter's hair
is not more dark than the cold wave
of anaesthetic which punctures
the illusion of deathlessness we carry
like an icon into each morning
no smaller than moonlight her quick hands
leaf into my face and dissolve as if
either of us were this nasturtium here
plucked and frozen in a photo like the secret
pain budding in her eyes which is so close
to love you can almost
touch it

# Cassandra

you walk the floor of a dead sea among
shrill bones the dust of plankton the piping
wind your near companion

alas alas for the towers of Ilium
vanished in the sediment teeth excrement hair
bloodied nails sinews bone echoes on the plain
where grass fattens on tongues churned to rot

no syllables avail you here
mute as the dead are mute

\*

you know
your death is nourished
in every place
harbouring your footprint

this your sentence

spoken always in a new argot
through the infinite declensions of Sparta
the first pure state

eye that sees only itself
bone unmarrowed of music
coward art that dulls
the bladed wings of freedom


its spawn in each unwindowed room
where worlds are scrubbed back to nothing


the inexorable bell
widens its silence
a bright wind flattening
buildings like grass
shivering us back
to the first sefiroth
nogod nobodaddy the jealously
concealed blasphemy


*

the limbs of a tree slide across the window
moved by invisible storm
as if one tapped urgently
as if to do injury as if to multiply fear
as if one sought harbour in a lighted place
an exhausted refugee from dreams
as if one were curious and conversational
and courteously sought attention
as if one were simply a tree
obedient to complexities of air
stirred by infinite intricacies
untraceable as the eddies of a mind
but immediately perceptible
in the movement of a finger
the unseen moving with clarity
in a tangible reality

in the pained
solace in the sweet disorder in the banishment
and meeting place the melts
wherein thoughts circle and grow muddy
anciently new or newly ancient
comforts spring

the curious tongue
might probe the fish of language to the bone
and never find motility nor the bright scales
scattered in the swamps of Ur
the calm eye anatomise having forgot its pulse
within a sea of tears -


so hands forget caressing
the haft in the palm the weight and vector of work
the word's multiple speaking in the flesh
nourished towards light

# The Edgeless Page

words I am heavy with words
a language glistens in my belly

unfolding all the old meanings
fresh and wet as an eye

it is curious as music
quickening the sensed invisible heart

learning the shape of its mouth
the way to push

through these softening walls
its whole inevitable voice

# Seduction Poem

I want the slew of muscle, a less
cerebral meeting place: no word
but your male shout, the shirred
unpublic face and honest skin
crying to me, yes,
the mouthless, eyeless tenderness
crying to be let in.

Unbutton all your weight, like a bird
flying the night's starred nakedness:
put down your grammatical tongue, undress
your correct and social skin:
come blank and absurd
all your language one word
crying to be let in.

# Fairytale

She was a wing heavy with no substance
love slumbered deep in her hollows
awaiting the hurricane of petals
and the sleeping poisonous dew
and the fabled sky unfolding
to the astonished vagrant
a realm of ivory gods and architectures
of apples and bees and harsh rivers

shrieks and caresses consumed her
she ladled patience from her shrinking marrow
the torrents of her hair
fell endlessly in mute pools
where eyeless fish swam invisibly
through spines and fangs to a blank gullet
and she drank waters bitter and tasteless
and cold outside the spectrum of touch

the windows were attentive
smelling her blood her scattered hands
all the white hours they looked and looked
and her eyes dwindled
outside were a city of judges
a burnt forest a mouldy fountain
broken girders a hairless doll and dogs
barking in the black implacable wind

# Sonnets

I

Let me say without self pity, that I love a man
who loves me more than sanity can bear,
who's so afraid, he will our love abhor
and give to others most of what is mine.
What of his cock? What of his private kiss?
They're mine, by right of pleasure and of pain,
and should he prick his gentle braille upon
another's flesh, how blind is my caress
which reads him true, and feels within his eyes
fidelity more deep than his betrayal.
But when the hearing opens on this trial,
my evidence is this: no man may use
my being so, and be himself untrue: and if he lies,
he lays his life aside, to both our loss.

**II**

When all is lost, the truth is strong as pain.
You woke my sleeping soul to living fire
and set desire raging where before
a timorous chill set numbing limits on
my pleasure's habitation: and fiercely I came
to edges of myself where no self had been
and felt the membranes split as I was born
fully into my life. If we have come
now to the point of parting, I dare this thorn
deny its sweaty rose: no bitter list
of wrongs elides this point; nor can our last
and ugliest words erase from memory my then
yielding and unyielding breath, which now
has found its shape and breathes itself anew.

## III

This baby in my arms has eyes like yours,
his hands are starfish miniatures of those
that cupped my tightening breasts, his rebel thighs
kick at the welcome light. In eighteen years
he'll be your mirror image. Because you buck
the burden of his fathering, I must learn
through his clearer compass how the lean
months of navigation will guide me back
to love. Unhusbanded, my loam unturned,
I'll make a bitter blessing of my sweat.
Our baby is like you, but in his sweet
body is a soul which shall be tuned
to joy, as yours to anguish, and I swear will live
fearlessly in light and, fearless, love.

## IV

Nor can I breathe, without the trust of breath:
nor can I speak, but for the listening ear:
nor can I wake, without the dreamless hour
which limns our bodies and divides us both:
nor can I rage, if you contain your ire:
nor can I weep, but knowing that you grieve:
nor can I die, without our common grave:
nor can I be in love, but that you are:
the breeze that floods us in its tenderness
is but a storm relaxed: the earth that now
repletes us with its fruit is one we know
already in unyielding winteriness:
in paradox our warring lusts align:
coupled at last, at last we are alone.

# Sonata

I

Almond blossom smears the dark
with its agony of promise: those white lips
fear no bruises, pushing out from the wet
gnarled branches that own their clumsy grace
to the rain, to the wind, to any who will listen
to that language without speech, which is always
sap burning through limbs that seemed dead,
urging the pitiless breath

solitude that flays the skin from my shoulders
o anguish at evening when the light
scars a landscape of shadows

in this living night
you are alone: I hear your cries
dismembering my soul with memory: the night
severs us, who always were alone: the flowers burn
down the length of my arms and my hands are empty.

## II

Water, ancient home,
formless tongue, abeyance, singing
out of the wordless world. Only to listen
flowering branches blaze in the sky and fill
our windows with liquid roses,
a child rolls into sleep, stars
fix in the eye's black distances –
only to listen, untouched by the grief of words,
which are not branches, which are not light,
which escape through faltering lips, and vanish.

## III

A bird is singing in the tree of night
its five-note song, and roses burn in darkness
outside the window where our children sleep.
In the house of my soul
the bed is smooth and dark, its pungent shadows
breathe in the empty room we still inhabit
and silently a book opens its voices
in the late air, where hands have been
waking to tasks, to the patient business of living.
All is quiet now, the light is gentle, and you,
voice that I love, o you are coming home.

# Angels

the night embodies them, they come
        with patient animal eyes
asking why it is we have forgotten them:
        pushing their childish mouths against our numb
mouths, parching with the loss of them:

the violent clouds announcing them, the bloom
        of carnal waters and the cries,
abrupt and wordless, which presented them:
        they are yet present, rumoured wings in rooms
where doors and windows shudder shut against them

# Failures

I was awake early when the sky was dark
and a hunger nagging me like the smell
of something I'd forgotten.
Maybe it was a siren in the distance
or the face of a woman I saw running
through the autumn shadows calling a name,
a year ago, two years ago, who asked me
have you seen him? have you seen him? have you?
But I had seen nothing.

# A unicorn

each thing we are given is like glass it is almost invisible we do not have the knowledge to hold it and it drops onto the ground and without knowing why we are bereft

this unicorn for example you might hold it in your hand you might say it is a lie because it does not exist and it is perfect as it is entitled to be because it does not exist

even your gasp of astonishment might shatter it even the timbre of your dreams even a glance might unwittingly and the unicorn is gone as if it were never there

and you feel the loss because although it didn't exist it was real

later we might be wiser but by then everything has already happened and some have forgotten even that who is to say they are unlucky

others however hold a mourning as if they nourished a tiny gravestone

where something might have opened and shiningly refracted them but that the agony of beauty split them back

entirely themselves and wholly lost

# Names

*for Ben*

the beautiful trains go in and out of his eyes
their names are pure, like the night in its bottle
fanning galaxies on his dream-itchy tongue

when he stands up the names come nuzzling
for pats and admonitions, he puts them in corners
and watches them swell until they burst into questions

the morning's percussion slides as gently as commas
through spoons and tables and arms saying no and yes
and nothing is sad, not even the sparrows
that prop and peck and vanish in the sky

# On the First Period after Pregnancy

it is so long since last I saw
this red familiar smut
I wonder what live thing in me
diminishes

I see now
how strange a thing it is to bleed
every month my tissue melting
and patiently rebuilding itself -

no wonder
the churches shudder: this blood
renews itself without sacrifice
and pours from no wound

it is the offering itself
naked of ritual
the generous ooze of wholeness
a tending of the valleys
where children grow

# Small Things

> *I worry for the small things*
> – Raising Arizona

those with teeth and thick skulls
need no advocates.
their fists are dumb machines
smashing the earth,
clumsy with the insolence
of wounded giants.
everyone knows
when the sly world plots
and slides a flat blade
through their shouting skins

and those with flexible tongues
they can look after themselves.
they use words like dangerous toys
spinning a beam of colours
into a white shield.
pain stares in its blank slant
and goes away empty handed.

but small things can't argue
their way into shelter
when the world explodes on them
implacably as stars.
they have only feathers
for the hurricanes
and thin leaves for the fires.
when bulldozers eat their houses
they squat on the edge of valleys
with nowhere to go.
the world is too mean for trust
but generous enough for murder.
It's getting worse. I worry
for the small things.

# Of prayer



words that want to summon a common awe
like the masked actor burning under lights
whose most artful gesture is burdened with innocence


as is the dusk seen falling on a flat earth
pregnant with the mystery of all objects
that obey laws imperfectly understood


and which cannot finally be measured
by even the most precise calculations:
and this deficit is with or without meaning


but either way of no matter to the birds that settle
to their shaded branches or to the beasts that wake
or to the sea rising on a deserted shore

# Wars

1

children played in the street
as if night were a little boy running
closer and closer

2

the terrible angels
flare out of the desert

no rain no mess
everything is simple

3

she is the scrawl
in the hidden book
she crosses the river
where no one is looking

she hates with the passion of a child

she will never grow up
the trees in her face
are still burning

# Translations from Nowhere

*A hard wing brushed past you, touching your hands
but to no purpose — this was not your card.*

*Mottetti*, Eugenio Montale

**1**

I cannot read my heart
it is a reticence
on the brink of invasion

the leaves of springtime shiver
under a metal sky
brushed by wings of wire

tangled musics
sweeter and more fierce
than hands can manage

**2**

because a day
is made of such different things
shining and avarice
many possible swords
the dust in my hair and the petals
falling from a wet sky


because every day
comes after another day
as if past and future
actually exist
and all the people I have been
sadly and beautifully dissolve
into amber, amber


there is no way back
deep in the sky
another wound opens
wars heave their famines
over every child
and all the leaves are singing
of the strange weather

**3**

I score such rightness
as does not come to me
easily

troubled
sap, a thrill of negation
opening on plenitude

a blank
light shapely in a doorway
held, stilled

woken
the hard eye
that does not blink

petalskin that ripples
under rain

shivering
without expectation
towards a tenderly

bruised sky
huge and animal and closer
as breath made

word and unmade

**4**

Whatever drags downward, the heart hampers:
          hands softer than dough
may leaven massy weights, o delicate
             knucklings of love

those confusing perfumes, wafers taken
          out of the fragrant ovens
to be laid on muteness, on whatever starves
          in crowds of noise

or between walls neither silent nor friendly
          where restless shadows
take refuge from themselves, wherever
          no rains fall

there may the tongue flood and flower:
          harsh the stone that cracks
the seed, harsh the fire, harsher still the heart's
          voiceless need.

**5**

that which is felt is felt
    beyond reason but not
beyond sense and may
        after all evade
both will and mind
    as a hare
may slip into cover
        before the very noses
of the hunt
            a truth
    blinking in dark foliage
hearing its own blood

**6**

the longed for is reticent:
shadows of wings or leaves,
light on a table


at evening when the heart
soars for reasons it cannot know


lips, words, o nothing
kissing the rim of day
with its bright absence

## 7

birds are gathering silently
along the rooflines
>   *leaping and returning*
>   *in restless circles*

even such squabbles as entertain them
evaporate in the feverish sky
>   *it is as if a doom*
>   *clouds over them*

inevitable as the soft night
who is a small boy running up the street
>   *when he reaches the end*
>   *the game is over*

then lovers leave their blood
to cool on the stems of briars
>   *the lame king closes the shutters*
>   *against the wasteland*

only children remain
listening to the silence
>   *until whatever swells in them*
>   *bursts open*

will the nightingale spring up
alone over the darkening roof?
> *will the children speechlessly*
> *run through the door?*

who is this word which approaches
from the white horizon?
> *they cannot tell*
> *longing from dread*

8

you know how the ice
                breaks almost casually, revealing
    those black gaps of water
                    that are reflectionless
    and of unknowable depths


it breaks and there is nothing
                to be done, the ice breaks
    in its own time according to the secret
                    fractures that were written there
        when it first formed


    it breaks and the water
fountains up, a white disaster
               catching the murderous sunlight
    that has shone so gently
           for ages now
patiently finding its music
    unpicking bitter patterns
            to their crises


and looking down from these heights
    how silent it seems
        suddenly, a deafness

silent as flowers that open
                painlessly overnight, their sudden perfume


     a pretence at coldness
but nippled in each centre, that tender pink
          unafraid, and further in
     something like an eye
or a wing

           something impossible

**9**

An ardour in the wind, flowers
thickening into spring. Thaws
afflict the mind, rivers of disaster.


They step, thin, lyrical,
out of the birches, they stand shining,
their footprints dark behind them
breaking the frozen grasses.


As if a myth had suddenly spoken
everything went silent, the sun blazed
silver, an intensity of motion,
the thrill of a knife cutting


then and now or the sudden
fall of a hawk, a shadow lapped
and vanishing in water, an eyelid
snapping open, dazzled full.

**10**

surely you were here before, somewhere before you
a goodly earth you'd heard about in stories,
a justness that eludes you now, a half-heard song

who said the word that led you here, what is this knife
that cuts and cuts, a radio breaking the distance,
or is it the trees again, how they deliver
precise dissections of sky, but never a stillness, always

the world, naked as usual, thick with meaning,
and now it makes you so weary, how it dissolves
like eyes in water or the trees that sing by the white road
moving and moving their dead branches

something led you here, it must have grown
out of a word, a moment, maybe how the light
fell on your hands one evening as they lay, bereft of law,
outside you, a tender yellow light without horizon

and you stared at a cup on the table, which was suddenly heavy,
the traffic too loud in the twilight, or was it some slow
forgetting, a burden that one day filled you
with hopelessness you hadn't known was yours
until it claimed you, your dumb double, grinning
as it beckoned you, you didn't know

and you stumbled into this light which is like blindness
someone put the road here but left it empty
only the crows are alive, shaking the trees
with their heavy ironies, maybe they watch you
idly, but they are going on with their own business,
as someone somewhere switches off the radio.

# Pain

sometimes pain seems to be the truest thing there is
it sits behind your eyes like a shivering animal
whose vision is a foil wretched with reflections
even skins are razors luminous with unshed blood

and you understand anew the fragility of touch
how real and clumsy it is, a derailed train
where bodies burst and shudder and collide
discourteously

                                      - there is no time
for pain's midnight pollen drifting through your veins
rooting and flowering into hallucinatory lymphomata

for shuttered lids and tongues tasting of metal
for the impotence of a half formed gesture that gutters out
and leaves a trail of rust inside the stilled hand
for the clarities which ripple in its silence

# Colours

There are colours you can only touch
Years ago I walked
Eyelessly through a black mountain

The sky shimmered like a knife
Poised to cut my breast in two
I remember the men in white

How they loomed over their instruments
And doors which opened and closed
I wondered if darkness was soft

Or if it felt like a collision
I wondered if I would wake up
Unable to shape my name

Locked inside my death
With hands as formless as gravel
The last thing I remember

Is the colour of kindness
My heart floating warm and strange
Through the chilling veils of my flesh

And someone took my hand and held it
And led me like a child
Into the dark

# Beauty

I have talked of beauty
I have held it
between these hands
always
without expectation
and always
as if I didn't deserve
such punishment

# The beast

The beast flies in the wind.

He is absolute in his terror. All myths, legends, tales, histories, rumours and superstitions cluster on his back.

We have seen him as a dark speck in the sunset on clear afternoons and pointed him out to our children. They regard him with a distant curiosity.

It must be admitted that he is decorative in the smoke and fire of the oil refinery. He gives a certain elan to the skyline. When he comes down to feed in the great houses of the land there is a flurry of obsequies and the presses stammer everywhere, shaking the earth.

It is true, nevertheless, that even the great cannot look him in the eye. He is a master of all language. The truth shrivels to whimsy in his gaze. He juggles ideas like baubles and the crowds gather, shouting and cheering. Children creep out of the shadows and watch, hypnotised and afraid, as his breath ignites the meadows of their innocence. The young men shake their fists and turn machineguns on the crowd, but no one notices.

The odd thing is that no one can remember what he looks like. His identikit picture illuminates our televisions but it merely resembles everybody else. Comedians lean towards their audiences, suspecting he is concealed in the raucous laughter. Old men lie in soiled beds and imagine they are consuming his ground remains in the pap spooned into their ruined mouths. Mothers cry out in their dreams. But everyone remains convinced that once they saw him, if only they could remember where. On a stage wearing a false moustache. Riding a white horse over a road gravelled with ashen bones.

He chucked a swaddled baby under its chin. He stood on the pipelines and yelled for more. He held a pen in an ornate building and bent towards the microphone. All his life, Goya attempted his likeness.

The current argument is that he doesn't exist. But we have all seen him. And we all know how difficult it is, in the smoke and drift of dreams, to find reliable witnesses. How small people are! How petty! How they crouch over their miserable campfires, howling for home! For they imagine that if they find their homes, he will be there cooking a hot supper and warming towels. If they looked up, they could see his belly trawling the air, gross, stinking, endlessly inflatable. But how is an ant to look at a mountain? And how to avoid his eyes?

It is, of course, an immense problem. Such voyagers as we have sent out come back with partial reports, if they return at all, and there are fewer and fewer volunteers. As science expands, our task is hammered down to arithmetic. Our wings are furnished with lead. Our vision is reduced to conundrums of optics. Our speech is a mess of splinters. Nevertheless, it is time to begin again, to plunge unwisely over this unidentifiable cliff into this many-coloured wind, which buffets us with the voices of the dead.

# All that nature

All that nature
Just lying around

I used to wonder
What it was for

It gets in the way
Or is simply dangerous

You have to
Put your foot on its neck

And stare straight
Into the camera

# Some steps

first into the eyes of lovers
who have not forgotten
how easily they are broken

secondly into the cradles
where children are abandoned
as offerings to silence

thirdly into the desert
where a prophet's skin
hardens into violence

fourthly into the house
where the dogs were shot
maybe first, maybe last

fifthly, pause at the idol
which has become invisible
and much more dangerous

# Songs of a dictator

**1: He woos his mistress**

you spoke too freely and too often
but your silence irks me
the world spins on your oyster


I have seen the future of civilisation
in the dry cemeteries of fanatics
serenaded by bulldozers


I cannot restrain my melancholy
the flunkies eddy in the corridors
and I'm sorry that I shot my fool


if you place your head in my oven
I will roast it for you
and all the birds will rejoice


even down to the estuary
where hungry swans
squabble in the oil

## 2: He regrets his youth

I often demanded that clean kiss
seldom has a man been more satisfied
but if it be permitted to ask

o jesu out of all bounties
in a life which has been unusually fortunate
to ask again for my innocence

as a young man imperilled, the first
gasp of power in the cornfield
when I bent her neck back and she weakened

suddenly against me and later
it was the ease of the gesture
as he collapsed in the dust, that astonishment

before it staled and the subtleties
of meetings in the palace or the barracks
revealed a carnal thrill, nevertheless

I sometimes wandered down to the chambers
to exercise my compassion and to flash
an avuncular epaulette

to some especially favoured or stubborn rebel
bleeding before his children perhaps
a pardonable vanity I think

now
it is all just a question for the lawyers who
superbly argue my desires

and no regrets in the face of my god
although I freely concede
I have no desire to meet him

## 3: His philosophy

hatred is for fools

we all know the truth
it is tiresome

words are better

I am patient
hence my longevity

the secret is
to fear everything

# Poems for Television

**1**

*The purpose of all coercive techniques is to induce psychological regression in the subject by bringing a superior outside force to bear on his will to resist. Regression is basically a loss of autonomy.*
- The Human Resource Exploitation Training Manual, CIA


a person's sense of identity
depends upon the continuity in
    his
        surroundings habits appearance
            relations with others
detention should be planned to enhance
    feelings of being cut off
from anything known and reassuring

    threat of coercion
weakens or destroys resistance
    more effectively
than coercion itself    the threat to inflict
    pain can trigger
fears more damaging
    than the immediate sensation
of pain
    if a subject
refuses to comply
    after a threat has been made
    it must be carried out    or
subsequent threats will
    prove ineffective

      pain that he feels he is inflicting
           upon himself i
s more likely to sap
          required to maintain
  rigid position   standing at attention   sitting
      long periods   the
immediate source of discomfort
                not the questioner but
          the SUBJECT
    subject
th sub
       exhaust     internal
motivational strength      intense        pain
      false confessions   fabricated
    avoid punishment

  unsettling       interrogation situation  ITSELF disturbing
         first timeenhanceeffectdisrupt
radicallyfamiliaremotional           psychological
    resistance   IMPAIRED   interval   suspended animation
psychological SHOCK   paralysis    traumatic   sub-traumatic
    EXPERIENCE      explodes    world
          familiar
   SUBJECT        image    HIMSELF    world
WORLDwrldwordwoewoewoewoe
         o o o o o o

    (at this moment the source is far likelier to comply)

# 2

    you get that bored
           it's **hot** the roosters
crowing up in the air condition'd
               Sub-Ordinated Perch of Power
this one that one wriggling those dollars
                     past the snoozing
     parliamentary heads o lordy
             THERE'S ANOTHER FREEDOM
we don't need to fight for any more
      because
  IT'S BEING PROTECTED
                  from us/for us it's

freedomfurnitureatdollarsavers
     baby baby baby      I *said* my eggs
are tired baby I said those wheels are **hot** I said
             the heat is like suffocating inside
    a chicken farmer's
*Boot*
                  so stunned you forget to notice
     that those people
       just got in A BOAT
and practically swam all the way to the *Cape of York*
                feral trees the jungle
     bleeding soldiers
*sendem to Weipa weepers* they said
     it was guns but we gottem
   offshore luckily they said **guns**
but *we know* that) in Irian Jaya

they're protecting the miners or
maybe it's **Certain**
**Maritime Arrangements** I get confused which
sea was that? it's hot
there too upstream or downstream it's all revenoo
under the sea or maybe chickens
getting hot and fluey
under those damn lights
they get so sweaty in them containers not to mention
the FILTH you gotta
midway or wake them if gitmo don't squeeze past
the signing statement we said
the DEFENCE OF SUPERIOR ORDERS WILL GENERALLY BE
AVAILABLE (*Nuremberg*) thank God
thank God thanks **GOD**

# A Requiem

**Introit**

> *Cassandra: Useless; there is no god of healing in this story.*
> - Agamemnon, Aeschylus

that crowd of ears
scurrying past the screams and brutal metal

through shivering walls the street talk burns us
none pity not one

I who policed my murder
and now I write my shame

but my wife went to the trains
but my daughter dies in my dreams again and again

how meekly I bargained with death
who will live to spit on my ashes?

through the wire her face emptied
my wife said nothing

\*

slagged by war you stare a thousand fathoms


a word
a shard of song
a leaf
the linking odour
missing


her white throat sliced open
her black panic smoking on the stone
dragging you here


silenced nevertheless
or nevertheless unheard
or nevertheless muttered at knee height
to erupt through the bronze talk of weapons


you step
towards the fatal palace


longing for the gilled sleep
before the appalled womb spat you
into this shattered hall of mirrors

this the gate of love
and this of hatred

this the mouth of offense
and this of healing

this the portal of dream
and this of disenchantment

this the long farewell
and this the endless greeting

## Dies Irae

> *so light is the urging, so ordered the dark petals of iron*
> *we who have passed over Lethe.*

> Canto LXXIV, Ezra Pound

I stand in the door of my house
I walk through its sleeping rooms
I number the beats of its breath

my hands brush
the shaft of a knife
the edge of a bowl of fruit
my daughter's tangled hair
the hair of my husband

animals that each night
embrace me with their scent
hands that clasp my neck
mouths that devour me

o livid planet pocked
by the veneration of wars
you are not innocent

\*

The child lay in his bed buttoned up for sleep
his hands folded under his head like a little boat
and I lay next to him on the raft of his breathing

All I could feel was the cold ocean under me
so deep that at the bottom no currents moved
the light bones that lay there

A steady vapour of fear drawing me closer
to the green water's unreflecting surface

\*

We toy with silence, that seductive bell - pouring its molten alloy into the pit of ourselves, holding our breath for the unflawed pitch - but the world is loquacious. How many voices are we?

How impossible to be rid of desire for a pure rebellion! What to do with that angel who boots me towards the absolute?

Yet cunning cloaks us with reason. We press the button out of spite.

\*

This is utopia dreamt by the burnt visionaries

These are their hells where the pale rider pauses at his calculations one third and one third and one third and one third the infinite divisions

This is the pit of human skulls and these are the trinkets of ears and teeth and here are screams in amber the prettiest of all

This is the hydra hand that breaks into millions and this is the one voice pricing the fruit of equations this is the mouth that gobbles the sweat of slaves this is the suit and the restaurant

This is the blinding cloud of ash the revolting unstoppable flower

This is the one just man who died on the final day of a war that never finished

\*

the cloth is rent and the table is split and the appletrees are blackened
           and broken
and the cradle is tipped and broken in the roofless bedroom

the sniper flicks a last cigarette into his stinking burrow
daughters and sons return to cities that no longer see them

the chapel is stained with foreheads pressed into their own blood
bindweed creeps on the empty roads like a child afraid of the light

and daffodils sneer in meadows that behave as if nothing has happened
bursting from sleep to bless the mildest of skies

though bootless feet stopped at their rims to flower
in greens and blues and purples that signalled the end of exile

the earth is indifferent as usual
dissolving coffinless children far from their cities

\*

what moves through light and water?
o laughter and night
and what comes after

what a violin's lone voice
might illuminate
with its pitiless

liberties, a tree's lost forest
axed into the flight
and warp of sorrows

a burned and chiselled violence
to amplify the bright
desolate silence

## Offertory

>*Praised be your name, no one.*
>*For your sake*
>*we shall flower.*
>*Towards*
>*you.*

>Psalm, Paul Celan

the dreaming boy hears in his pillow
mad echoes of hoofbeats

the heart of Varus is eaten raw
his head grins from a stump

the trees blanch like a scream
untimely ended

\*

the citadel is not taken
the citadel was never there

the beautiful Europeans
scribbled the earth with churches

they believed the text was immortal
and God heard their singing

who is to say they were wrong?
in the middle of nowhere

blue irises bulb
from the eyes of the dead

•

one candle bleeds enough warmth
to keep a body breathing

in the coldest
emergency

although the mind may be damaged
by the constant repetition

of lighting one candle
again and again

*

a man is weeping in an alley of stone
the alien ground thickens with his noise

to his fathers it was a desert
and his mother is buried far away

and he doesn't know what angers him
or why his tears seem a refusal of blessing

except that at last something is clear
that he should have known before he left

when the household gods flew out
and the door swung shut behind him

\*

who is asking questions?
throw them out

where is the ancient song?
forget it

what violets slumber still?
possess them

lock up safe
swallow the key

\*

the night's small teeth
ate my hands and my hair

I was a pebble of faith
the moon's little sister

storm blew open the door
but no one could find me

\*

the hand that touched you through the words
that wrote the words that vanished in their saying

the mind that stroked the hands that moved
the lyre that sang the words into silence

the night that opened in the heart that sang
that opens in the night that is endless

\*

yellow star the trench is deep
that cowls your shyness


birches whiten as the spade
unveils your hair


your eye opened and closed
the day stalks in


a blaze of witnesses
to consecrate your absence

# Communion

*I show you a new world, risen,*
*Stubborn with beauty, out of the heart's need.*

Taliesen 1952, RS Thomas

My flesh is sad with itself, it walks in the garden
heavy and opaque, an insoluble riddle.
The bruises on my arms are lightening
and a dew softens my mouth
as birds wink in and out of the trees.
But still I am sad.

The oranges are pale moons. The wind
sings them into eclipse and calls them
back from the black leaves.
I envy their voicelessness, the sweet
fertility that falls
mindlessly to the grass.

I am not gentle tonight.
Tonight my calling is useless,
betrayed and foresuffered. If my face
chills in its blood, if my eyes startle open,
it is because all this sobbing will fall
to inhuman water.

They will say they are redeemed.
They will crown my absence with their suffering.
But I remember a crowded table
and a plate heaped with oranges
and how generous hands reached out and tore
open the common flesh.

# For Ben

Child, the world is swelling, light wavers
over your unblinking eyes, the ocean lifts you
on dark mouths towards the sudden dawn
when you'll howl the sea out of your lungs
and harden in the air.

To welcome you I have these eyes and fingers
to open their delight on your sundered skin.
They'll fail, as all desire fails, breaking on the reef
of human weariness and gathering past
its violation to simplicity

perhaps. Here is the cushion of my blood
and there the grail of sobs with which I'll bear you.
These breasts will weep for your innocent greed
and bring the void of solitude and your first fears
stalking you like witches.

Yet still I wish for you an inexhaustible love,
the fruits of every season, a sure voice to name them,
shelter when you seek it and the sixteen winds
to call you from yourself back to this first ocean
and further to the wider ocean.

# Notes

numb
anemone heart
clawed into a dumb roundness

flinching deeper than grief
where even dreams
cannot touch

no place to speak
and now all places have vanished

the mouths closed over the dark mouth
closing over them

\*

there is courtesy in how you greet me
and when we meet we are still reticent
understanding now there are wounds
words will smart against or numb but never heal

in our hearts twist inherited hatreds
which have already throttled love for us
and yet we touch

\*

the angle of your face
>                between my thighs -
>                                the thousand notes
>                                                of your lucid tongue -


the taut fruits
>                                        shivering to wakefulness
>                against my lips -


o trees may embrace
>        as slowly and completely
>                        the solemn earth
>                                and the unquenchable light
>                                                and know the joy of sap
>                                sweetly engorging them -


>                        but music once
tore their roots with listening
>        and eyes rustled open
>                        blindly after Orpheus -
>                                                that instrument of
bone
>                                scoring the blank sky
>        with worlds of loss -


>                        its blood foaming
>                in the breath
>                                of angels

\*

who was going to save you
pretty bird o love of mine
the moon fell into pieces
the rain was not a sign:
the air was full of noises
the clouds were sudden bruises
and when you tried to make them sing
they broke and all the stars came in
and none of them had faces:
and then your blood was strange to you
bristling inside your skin
and strange the lidless eye which burned
your insides out to empty sky
and nothing spoke from that abyss
and no one held your hand:
o how you longed for sleep then
little bird o love of mine
the blue horizon split and bled
across the desert of your bed
o how you longed for sleep

\*

madness
is love broken
by its loneliness
is desire broken
on the tongue of lust
is the mirror broken
where the self hides
and the broken mind
screaming for silence
and the broken hands
panicking for rest
and the broken eyes
admitting nothing
and the broken heart
breaking

\*

your subtle lips
prick stars out of my skin
voluble as laughter
shivering the darkness


perhaps you called I am already here
unravelling like speech in our shining dreams
lip on lip spelling us stranger
unlocking all the beasts of our tongues

\*

little delicate animal
your thin shoulders press against my belly
the bones of your face stand out like an adult's
and your neck that white naked stem
is laid across my thigh
as if I could protect you

\*

my window
prickles with old stars.
a door shuts. children
run in their dreams

beyond the foggy
pastures of psychology:
my breath whitens
to silence

\*

Whose was the hymn of making, who clapped open my eyes, whose was the blood which layered me lip after lip, prism of words, swarm of enticements, asylum of hair - I looked in my heart's strongbox and all the arguments shredded there do not muffle her voice - I leaned down and she whispered her litany of revolution -

    which always returns me to this still place

    the breath of my children - they are not grateful but they love me - they teach me to expect nothing - they restore me to many things I lost: a stone trough filled with miniature flowers, the privacy of nests in bamboo thickets, a tiny lawn always filled with the voices of books, a blue gate -

    Perhaps this is simply what I wanted to tell you - of these webs of love shivering in the emptiness -

# What the Glove Said

I am silken and wholesome.

Sometimes in the night I am seen shaking.

Jackals bay in the littered alleys but I pay them no mind.

I am concerned with the skin of nearness.

Between one tooth and another, the iron passivity.

I disgorge hands and sleep. I eat and wake.

Such prey as use me never tell their names.

I am fond of wordless proverbs.

Love is a roof of rain and a habitation.

Such tears I wipe would stun the bilious world.

My dance is with the air.

I hide and disclose like a poem.

# Bird

The bird is
a deep and troublesome fidelity.
Even as maggots crawl through its braincase, it is still bird.
In the skirl of storm
it is bird, torn feathers, tiny bones,
breasting the weight of air.
Its song pricks out the present
but is the shape of itself, the whole heart-trembling arc
of its small time.
It persists through winters and summers,
never less than bird.
If it knew any better, I would call it courage.
Somewhere beyond me
is a wholeness, a memory of being stone,
although this consoles nothing and explains nothing.
The dark is a burning sky
shot with flight, its solitary, naked love.

# Prologue

You'd better start, the sun said
As I lay blinking

My manners were arrested
By surprise

It's not good enough, he said
Even I become tired

Of going up and down again
And sometimes wish to find

A dark lover to hide in
But where I am there is no night

And no one to complain to.
Abashed, I began.

# Untitled

there bees were perpetual as meadows asleep in a brooding sun
or a curlew recalled as a mirror of all sadness


no one could tell if it was day or night
they always slept on the silk of their delusions
wherever they fell
in the dust of libraries or among the soft
vegetations of sensual musings


no one was certain either of borders
and therefore the citizens were courteous to strangers
continually puzzled by familiarities
as if they were siblings raised in the same hayfield
or perhaps cousins suckled on the same wolf
as if the face before them chimed
like bells on an alien planet


they were too shy to compare fingerprints
it could have been that each whorl matched exactly
and so their harmonic voices
drifted through the grasses like a cloud of questions
waking lizards and beetles from innocence
and the flowers hastening after rain

but every now and then a citizen would wake
with a phrase in her head that she couldn't explain
and found the libraries were silent

then she would walk through the humming streets
past refineries and docklands beyond the knowledge of cities
until she found a rock inhabited by no voice
perched on a mountain with no history
and there she would breathe an air without language
pure and violent as a galaxy

and only then would the veins in her feet
tell how cold the ground was and how bloodless

how unlike death
which laboured hotly in those other cities
she saw teeming beneath the torn sky
so far from the home she could never return to
now that it never existed

# Cuneiforms

red fist, nose, coney, eye,
moody orchid,

dripping black,
viscous yellows, white

crumbles of honey,
weep, knowing death

is dry and the first voice
is water

\*

moontree, shaking out your moths
into warm currents

brushing here a harp, there
tympanies of skin

now a clutch, now a swarm,
now a flight of lips

constellations
flaring in the blood

\*

cunning lips, split
by your knowing

flesh-music, carnal
staves of labour,

the wet cry flourishing
and crumpled wings

burning
in the new air

\*

you, other
skin, unguessable

shape of my embrace,
a blue sail swelling,

vanishing, your familiar
hull heaving clear

of the dazzle of our
common sea

# Ars Poetica

It will make no difference.
But you'll find you can't speak without love
although it's an imprisonment.
Your voice must be love wrestled to unloving,
the lyre at the moment of catastrophe, a silence
within which another voice opens.

You'll speak as you must, as always,
although you'll never know why you're listening
through the elisions of your stuttering heart.
You'll long to finish, although nothing has happened,
although you haven't begun, as if your mere being
hurt you with abundance. No one will explain.

There are wounds that blind you, sudden voices
splitting into winter, toothed windows, terrors
sifting through white slumbers of corruption,
the wraith that greets you with your shrinking face
at dawn, anonymous and violent,
waiting for Virgil.

Because you have tasted your salt in the blood
of another's mouth, because a small flower
is eating the history of stone,
because you are asleep and all possibility
tilts on the edge of your vision, because you are nameless
and are called, because you know nothing -

a possible music
lifts through the panic of dismay -
it's the blue of all the flowers of your body,
the brain stem, the clitoris, the tongue,
the wrist vein, the channels of the heart, the dying lips,
reaching to their likeness in the sky, in the sky's waters -
you can't lift it out of your flesh
because it won't exist, but it flowers past you.
It opens the places you've always been,
house, fire, glass, bed, water,
tree, night,
the child's glance which strews your transparencies
across a field of colours you have no name for,
the profane ash of touch
darkening your tongue, the dream of imperishable silver
which wakes to another dream, a boat departing
from an unmapped shore, and your crumbling words, unable
to hold even one drop of light.

# Nights

I

In the circle of the night, the sun is burning.

The child squirms inside you, its eyes are open although it has seen nothing, no one has looked on it, it has no face.

Has it fed on your bitterness?

My body is eaten out. And this fragile crust, it has no face.

There is no judgement I have not thrown at the mirror. What then is possible?

My hands have lost courage.

## II

Out of sleep, monstrous swells of pain. Out of dark, the modest flame of a candle. Out of night, voices and hands.

Here, on this bed where I have suffered and loved most, he is born into his solitude.

I have no mask.

All I am is offered to the flame.

## III

The dawn breaks over your eyelid.

Immense flowers bruise your horizons.

Child, your single cry is the axis.

Your weightless burden filling our hands.

**IV**

Speech is so fragile, it is as if we have never spoken.

My hands have never been so shy. My face will not reveal the lucid wings inside me.

You cannot see me.

Moths inhabit my clothes. Rats inscribe the ceiling. The slow beat of living continues, intolerably.

I can't touch your pain. Its cold light spills through our sleep.

The rain is no longer a voice. It is merely the rain.

## V

He has no speech. He hungers and is fed. Darkness is a warm fumbling of lips.

The child's light is unfractured, he smells of milk and almonds. He reinvents the future as he sleeps.

I have too much to learn.

When you enter me I am a house without walls. I cannot enter you, or perhaps I enter you too entirely. I have no way of knowing.

Our language is a bitter struggle towards the child's speechlessness. We fail, always. What can return us to that first garden, when I flowered under your blind hands?

But I have watched your face, naked in sleep.

# Aubade

midnight rolls like hunger
into the still eye of an absolute dawn

all the possible birds arrive
and fly through your skin like music

# Divinations

**1**

You always spoke for me
so how could I name
what happened later

the earth was generous:
her rising hips
burned with flowers

and clouds darkened on her skin
summoning the springs
of an intolerable compassion

## 2

Returning, it seemed to me
that eyes bruised
against the dark of flesh:
that hands flaked to ash
in unsensed fires:
that now we stood
helplessly as strangers
locked in a season of frost:
a beat, a gesture, an eyelash
and the sky empties:
the word flies out
and is extinguished:
and everything is lost again
for the first time

**3**

The lovers pressed their cheeks
one against the other

skin bruising and dissolving
in a monstrous kiss

and each passed through each
into pure odour

birds, lung, bricks, trees
sliding into black water

**4**

What is this empty face?
this dry inscription?

these cold echoes splashing
on the floors of dream?

is there no kindness here?
no delivering hand?

this eye rots in sleep
this mouth opens

this heart walks unshriven
through its own winter

5

This hand was the flower on your mother's breast
rooted in the dark river
which winds into the day and vanishes
and it was the crucible
in which the sunlight hardened to a crystal
which glows still
behind everything you have forgotten

you have placed this hand with involuntary pity
along the cheeks of those you love
and felt the certain language break
like flocks of birds spelling out the winter:
a cold sky, a breast of twigs
which your voice inhabits, darkly
drawing to itself its own hunger

and nothing given you but this pressure
of light through your skin
to show how precisely your negations
add up only to beginning:
a mouth poised before the unsayable
an eye stricken by sight
an empty hand

**6**

You open the blue gate
in the wall of stone
and pass through the dense
birdhaunted forest

the rhododendron drops
its scarlet tongues
through the green heavy perfume
of rotting earth

and the branch which snapped
under your swinging thigh
is falling again
into the distant summer

7

In the simple gardens
the orchards of hair and sweat

mesmeric with apple and beehum
where birdbreath tunes its delicacies

and the skeined senses tumble out their embroideries
the eyed wing, the amphibian tongue, the feathered hand

stone loosens its speech

**8**

The swallows too are bending the light
calling the blossom out of the frost
with their precise magnetic eyes
and wings of articulate hunger

out of the panic and twittering
emerges the sun and the splitting cell
shapes an eye for its mirror

and children with voices of water
carelessly inhabit the light
time for them is a bird
piping its promise on the edges of sleep

where soon the reluctant ghosts will stand
like bodies of rain in the falling light
of a sunless garden

**8**

Dreaming, I woke up and left our bed
and pushed aside the arms of trees
bent with liquid kisses and I saw
the town where I was born as once it was
revealed in the clarities of childhood
as someone calling, far away, my name

then I saw you, but your hands
were flayed and burnt, your eyes gone,
your lovely belly torn and gaping
and your mouth a shadow within shadows:
and the church was broken, the school empty
and leaves blackened the square

the world bled around you as you called
stumbling across the frozen rubble
and then I was afraid, because you called me
into your darkness, and I followed you

**9**

A dog ran from the whistle a child tugged his mother's skirt
the dog skittered through leaves of rain a bird cowered the child chased the
       bird
the dog circled the twilight deepened the child hit his mother
the bird hid the moon was gibbous the jasmine swarmed through the
       deepening air


a nub burgeoned with lips and fingers sucking life through its eyes of water
voiceless fearless sunless wingless branching into my blood
the sky tripled its risk folding the clouds in joyous omens
o black foot o little finger of fear
innocent like a lash of hair pricking the hidden eye


who was the wolf who paced the bedroom scarlet tongued and ruffed with
       hunger?
who was the child which fell into the riddling cabbages?
who was the mouth which steamed a duff of lies in the fuzzy nights?
who was the word which stamped and stamped until all thoughts were its
       footprints?
who was the eye which broke and bled as it fell on the polished floorboards?
who was the finger wriggling in and plucking out god like a tooth?
who was the thunder cracking the roof until all houses were shadows?
who was the witch who marched up and down with her lonely hammer?
what was the body which knew no names a bloom of nerves a barb of
       questions?

**10**

I listened for you in the throat of summer, in the fanfare
of trees I lingered and spelt their shadows

you rose out of my darkest soundings, inaudible fish
eyelessly twirling in warm currents

autumn cauled your arrival, tracking my veins with weariness
and floated you out on sad leaves of blood

down to the icy waters where gentle fingers
will never prise into bloom your promise

and my kisses will never spark your hair
joyously into brief unknowable beauty

nor will the eager petals of your skin
char to brutal seed

## 11

We wake up from what is endured
patiently, without hope, and find
that old hunger waiting with its pinched face
and radiant eyes. Nothing will drive it away,
it will simply transform
and implore us again. What can be done?
It cannot be fed and yet it begs us
and hurts us, like an angry child,
and there is nothing to eat.

Poor fruit, these windfalls
rotting in the garden of love.
They swamp the mouth with death.
Remember, once there were apples
confusing the sky with pure savour.
Remember, the thighs of saplings
interrupted the air's foolings.

The ghost of a child
lingers and its wan voice
has no language.
It nags us like an old grief
which will not lessen and no tears
will silence its complaint
chiming out of the shadows
in this torn place:
which never shall be
and never was

**12**

*(for Rilke)*

You spoke out of that deep cleft,
sexed and unsexed, where carnivorous petals
caress the strangeness of dream -
but what nocturnal meetings
deliver you here, emptied so finally of yourself,
poet whose gaze was self


o cruel love, coldly tended in solitude,
forcing out of the chilled root
its delicate bloody garland:
and night moves through you, inhuman, voiceless,
bleakest of gods, deaf
to the continuously dying self delivering
its first and only cry


and the gladness in your being
grows tired and folds itself away
and all the names you mine out of silence
retreat into the sounds of themselves
and the earth raises its horizons
so close to your mouth you cannot speak
and the roses shut before your fingers
alien, innocent, illegible

and you fall towards the dark
unwinding genitals and tongue and eyes
to feed the faceless wind that scours you:
for who can say what ripens
tenderly in stone, or what flames
sleep beneath black water, or what mouth opens
its articulate springs after the last
songless winter

# Nude with mirror

He could no more perceive her than touch his own horizon
retreating before him over cliffs of reason,
and she knew this and became bitter.

No wonder she stared so long at her own reflection
scrying the despair of one unlooked at
who so became nothing, and yet was there,

inclining to death, a lack refashioned as lust
purely to be granted or withheld, and perhaps a lost
distorted gleam of unimagined gardens,

delirious fabrics stretching out in sunlight,
cities of colour exhaling conversation
where a childish greed might be abashed

to luminous admissions. She will undress
only to a nakedness apparent to his sight,
abandonment more brutal than her silence, it is enough

to catalyse his nuclear hatred. Does he flinch
at her caprices? She must put on the garments of a mother
and ladle him to earth, droplet by droplet, before his fear

evaporates and once again he meets the querulous city,
neither shriven nor exorcised, and she
turns again in mockery to the mirror.

# Yet

yet it is you in the morning broken-winged angel
you imagined yourself in the fire or in the frost you imagined
how beautiful the arc of your fall how the wind caressed your cheekbones
how you hardened to steel how you smashed in the neon lights
like a bottle of petrol like the scream of an anguished guitar
yes you imagined all this in your infant sleep curled in the rose of your mother
        and the blue fatherly distances
you sang in the arms of trees and looked at such far horizons
the waters so blue the waters so brown the waters smoking in the dawnlight
the slumbering opal breast of an ocean of exile
o child you were so alone you were a breath of ice
exhaled through smog where flowers fell from your thighs and withered
the crimson petals of sex the stamens of boundless love the bitter pollen of
        words all fallen and wasted
in the mucous of sad afternoons the ash and decay of silent evenings in
        mornings of green despairs

and after midnight after the chimes rang out over the empty city square
you saw the hands of the clock running around and around and laughed
you were sick already with useless nostalgia you felt how the skins inside
        you twanged their hollowness
you wept in treacherous armpits you lay on your stinking bed screaming a
        name you sniffed the menstrual tears you tasted again and again the
        arsenic of shame
o angel the cold electrified your hair the stars fell trembling through your
        fingers you tongued the million bells of night there was nowhere you
        wouldn't fly for love

but your wings were already breaking
your spine snapped in two and four and eight you fell but not at all as you
        imagined
the jurors mocked your gracelessness and even then you couldn't weep
love dragged you from your icy dreams and broke you with its fist
the fist was bone and you were bone the million bells clapped shut inside
        your skull
and nothing rang back nothing nothing nothing

# Tracing the damage

when you imagine the moon
makes the edges shine

the world a naked place
where you place beauty
as if it were an artefact

no matter how gloriously the contours of your sight
expand in this impatient light

at the centre
numb white

\*

naturally it was always there
from the budding of memory

but now you simply float
you have seen it at last

this impossibly bright
silver pulsing
against the back of your eyes

everything else a red shadow
nudging you like a bruise

\*

as if you could eviscerate that silence
with a scalpel

as if it could burst like a septic finger
its evilsmell
rotting at last outside you

the clean wound
simply a matter of pain

\*

nothing is simple
you no longer know how to understand yourself

the word spoken in the circus
as a spinning body
dizzied by its own skill

an angel who approaches without courtesy
and spears you with his tongue

ah and after the consummation
what might be wished?

after the vigils and tears?
after the silence?

\*

you understand only
the shine at the edges of things

the wing of a blackbird
flicked from your sight

words that vanish
precisely when you need them

\*

somehow the blue is approachable
wished from your distances

hot evanescent
thrill of perception
slamming your eyelids open

your skin a fine net
tiny blue fish
flashing through

the violate
air gasped in

   yes

# Afterwards

*for Marina Tsaetayeva*

You can't hear your own voice any more.
The air is loud with geraniums and daisies
but you pass through more quietly than the rain.
You have no business with flowers or with the earth.
You have no business with the people hurrying past you.
You are still and hidden.
If you take a knife
maybe you can find yourself all the way in
and any action is dangerous
the cancer might blossom behind your ear
or the sky slide down and shatter.
Maybe no one is listening, but the walls are curious.
Maybe no one is watching, but the trees are attentive
and ripple with unseasonable winds.
You don't know when you will hear the knocking
so you stay awake all night, a flickering ear.
In the day you are as small as possible.
You wonder if the dead are still in pain
and if they dream, for you are forgetting to dream.
Already you are insubstantial as the corpse of a sparrow.
You can't even scream, you are empty,
you want to be empty, you want to feel nothing
because nothing can stop it.
When she visits you, you sit ashamed
fiddling with the cutlery. You have forgotten the formalities,
you have snuffed out the wingbeat of courage
or maybe it was never there. You study your mirror,
a white plate broken in the mud.

# They do not arrive in time

*No 52, The Disasters of War, Francisco Goya*

the ground is patient
it does not acquire hunger
only light

the stone is as patient as a hand
one stroke of black after another

the face might be lost in a sulk of sleep
but its heaviness tells otherwise

a black cowl pushes down the body
gripped by crude fingers

her white fingers hang

a few curved lines pull the dress
tenderly across her breasts and belly
she is still fresh

she is of course a crucified madonna
no doubt she was patient

for the rest, faces
living and dead

bearing witness

# In a restaurant

Of course, the real disaster is always one's own death. The immortal slave was seen dining with a merchant prince, archduke of the electronic dreamwaves, executor of sharemarkets, poker machines and two flies up a wall, potentate of the demesne of tittle-tattle, authority of virtual hope and manufactured despair, a man as sensual and fragrant as money, with a sleekness that purses the lips of prime ministers and minor tyrants in shrewd calculations.

It is not enough to make the world bow down with a toxic smile on its lips. But it may be some compensation.

# On the Death of God

In the age of barbed wire, they announced the death of God. Great men traced the flyspots on ancient walls and studied the mutations of stars. Never before was so much knowledge gathered together.

They forgot to examine the dirt at their feet which was, as it always has been, full of God. A vast emptiness winced at the core of things. They thought that if they stepped on the moon, the cancer would retreat. They thought that if they invented washing machines, the asylums would empty. They thought that if they wrote enough books, the poor would vanish. Nothing worked.

They became more and more afraid, and ordered inventories of their armouries.

To combat their anxiety, they wooed the drug barons of Burma and Mexico, the bankers of China, the potentates of Somalia and Wall Street, the despots of Indonesia and Chile and Uzbekistan, the monarchs of America and the Middle East. Many were photogenic and drew huge ratings, and white opium clouds soothed the people. But still they had forgotten God.

In the East, where God had been banished forever, the Pope rose out of the stills of the dispossessed and boxed the ears of the Kremlin. He raised his hands and God stepped forward to the podium. As they watched, a giant crow landed on the steps of Congress and plucked out the eyes of onlookers. A dark cloud hovered over Persia.

They understood then that God had never gone away. His transactions passed all understanding. Not a sparrow fell, but He sold it. He suffered the little children to come to His wars, and His dogma belched from all the world's leaders. His factories and powerstations obliterated borders and his mansions towered over the hovels of the unenlightened. The electronic nerves of every economy led to the bottomless abyss of His intelligence. Already it was too late.

# Enduring freedom

i

everything is different now
                                      apparently

      reporters are treated for trauma
because of the footage
                they don't show us

                        I remember the silence in the news room
        when the photos came through the wire
            of the gassed Kurdish families
and the children in Bhopal

                 they never got in the paper
either

(that was before photoshop
        cleaned up the foam around the mouth
of the pretty child airlifted
            out of the warzone
                    for surgery

our hearts bled at the kindness of us
                it was all part
of the wallpaper)

ii

history finished and then it started again
                with a 'new need for colonisation'
      and by gosh we get to try out
our helicopter gunships with those
                      whizzbang double shooters
      by gum by jingo by jesus
it's a real war we've got here
      and you kids you're all Good remember
Good always triumphs over Evil
            and it's real Good of you
to send your pocketmoney
                to Those Less Fortunate


so long as you play the right music
      the screens mist over with tears
and we dream our Heroes
striding over the wastelands
           with their swords erect
and their pockets full of antibiotics


in Guatamala you throw Evil into the sea
                    from an airplane
and in San Salvador you rot its face with acid
        and dump it in the streets
so the citizens will be properly afraid
      of Evil
           as it is liquidated by History

Africa's another story
            and then there's the Middle East which nicely
oils our Western Way Of Life
                just make sure you bring the white cash
    in on Cessnas
        to fund the War on Drugs
which keeps Evil gibbering in prisons
     and so on


       Evil we're all agreed
         is Evil
  and must be fought
      by every possible means


now it has a new face
        laboured out of the bowels
          of the Pentagon
so lovingly conceived and now lurching
    towards another bloody apotheosis


      you might notice
          the dark side of the skull
is green like money always has been

            but everything is different now


*October 18 2001*

# La Belle Dame

the lake looks inside itself
the sky has forgotten summer
and you there    white on the grass

I can watch you
from all these miles
although there is no sun
there is no sun at all

all my mouths sang for you
those long nights
and every word was true
the lake shuffled its visions
the stars trailed their bitter distances

what poison did I set in you
so lovingly
that this winter is a scythe of wails
that against me your luxuriant veins
flower to livid ash

# Rising from Aquifers

*Co-written with Sophie Mayer*

In the middle of the map they put Medea.
As if to say of the site DO NOT ENTER.
As if to admit how they had provoked her.

HAZCHEM: a warning almost invocation.
Lord of the poison, sacred their mission.
That nuclear familiar wasp-sting of a sign.

She: triangle or angular. She: triangulating
all causes, all histories, all laws and all lines,
infectious connections she chews to the horizon.

Late Old English *curs*, of unknown origin; no word of similar form and
sense is known in Germanic, Romanic, or Celtic.

rising from aquifers salt ghost vengeful
kinstrife betrayal voices persistent
crying out birth scars here's your physician

open cut mouth or slickwater microfractures
"reducing friction" right in the womb

take that motherfucker take that kidkiller
white ulcer written on living tissue
skulls in museums labelled in cursive

> An utterance consigning, or supposed or intended to consign, (a person or thing)

hashtag/gash/gulp/pulp
rape rape rape is an 'insult
to our [his] honour' is

> to spiritual and temporal evil, the vengeance of the deity, the blasting of

the sticking-of in is the politics
of take, saying 'virgin land' saying
peak oil Peak oil PEAK oil does it

> malignant fate, etc. It may be uttered by the deity, or by persons supposed

get you hot (like to wallow) follow follow
the shockwaves to swim in poison calling
leak at every turn, shale the safe stuffed

> to speak in his name, or to be listened to by him.

w/
nothing
but

> In its various uses the opposite of *blessing*.

                    sweet raintrickle through earthskin
                        whisper the dry through
                    wordmaps cave to cave place to place

                                    serpent blood
                            pooling in dark/worldthroat
                                speaking its slow song
                    living water living stone the upthrust living
                                    nets of whole

                            you take it in your steely hand
                                    saying 'mine'
                                        mine it

                under
                mine

                umber
                amber
                sand &
                ochre

                no
                yoke
                choke
                hold
                no
                'no'

aerial map the veins
>   break the vessel open
>       suck out the blood
discard the husk

>   songtalk lovetouch story
drying leaves in the wind
>       carcass fell & rot
>           and yet
still red still hot
lips still singing

>               shesong snaketongue to
>                   gather
>                   sweetgrass
>                   loosestrife
>                   lady's bedstraw

>               all our names lovegiven
>               all our names soft pretties
>               & complex experiment

>                   on our

lipstills(t)inging
the nettle of grasp/gasp/rasp/
but
>               sap rISing

# Owl Songs

**I**

she was made of flowers : named and shaped and punished

taken from her stemmed sleep : and slapped to eye

petal breasted whore : buddable and silk : soft orifice

his to hold and husband :  nectar swelled and stank : she split to claws

or so the story said
a long time ago
in another place

\*


what skin is. organ of music
edging self, places of rawness,
worldvoice shaking you to its distances,
running you through invisibly


\*

the broken can't be mended:
not sky smeared and stripped, not looted forest, not the algal river,
not cancered earth, erupted gene, memory extinguished,
nor starved shot scurvy fur and feather, nor the flamed
and thug-smashed home, nor shard shocked child-damage:

the faith in seed:
                     that green will burst the grey
carapace of ash
                            cover the bone-site over

\*

ash rose and rose of stone,
miraculous petals martyred from the wood
undoing bone as paradise pricks sight -
the lovely cheek, the leaf, the tear, unfleshed
past wail or weal, flashed to shadow:
rose whose secret petals close the harm
blent for public pap into the fearsong:
calculations of empire: tithes of blood.

\*

      the loosed weed lives:
      under her leaves
             rot ancient languages

      dragged into touch
      she cannot but scorch
             the sweetest seasons

      alien honey
      driving the shy bee
             into extinction

\*

      she the impediment
      of mind    a stutter
      masked with feathers

      she gulps your useless history
      and spits it out in pellets

      spelled
      by a speech with no words
      for the perfumes congealing
      on her mute lips

how harmless she looked!
but her tongue watered already
for what was missing


*


probing the iris, a laser
cuts all the way in
to the truth: a dead thing
leaking on the slab

**II**

What becomes conscience, shame mating with love
in the eye of a child driven to hurt.
It isn't your fault you were born.


So much missed, the womb's slow thud, the gentle light,
muffled mother music imagined as heaven -


but save the blame. No god will coddle you
back to that dimness. The light grows brighter and harder,
breaking your sight, breaking it into pieces.

\*

                    Symptom is all:
the king of wrong erases with a doctrine
evidence of death.
                      Love broods in the womb
flexing its fingers for the world's warm breast,
its cry of nails hammering the harm.

\*

matter moves as light
      a Rabbi wrote in Prague


           marking the golem
           zapped by godword
           slavish man-mock
           tricked from mud


    how we bettered that!
           petty gods, intellect's brazen angels
naming the strings of light


           how beautiful the equation
that blasts the feeling flesh


        a single hand
                      gestures and is ash:


        o smile, o kiss, o love,
    pain would not be but this,
        given and revoked, alas,
 r      evoked and given.


\*

there is nothing to understand

the flower dissolves into its secret
the holding eye revolts

war is a mask he can gobble everything

the earth panting beneath his feet
where he always wanted her

\*

the book the smirk and the hot rack
the bridle of spikes the bent foot
the stone the wheel the bar the law

beat them into a tongue
with both your hands

pretend the tongue is a flame
tend it gently

\*

wretched exile wrenching the wordhoard

*

rails vanishing into cold
she played with starlessness

Yes said the face in the window
I can hear you even behind the frost

*

eye, touchlight, bag of water, pinhole letting the world in,
look, mind not the how: be

                    wavelets shunting cell to cell
softly flaring mind
        the kiss of wind, branch
morphed to arm, gods whispering

eye blooded shut
                now open
yes?
        and whose the broken speaking
                yours?   mine?

                        soultrust violate
                  fingertouch
    a questioning of all edges
                          heart    numb
           wingsofblood


                me?           you?          me?

## III

relearning how to be still, that is the difficulty.
blinder and more coldly clouds race
far above the pious stone, which has nothing to do with you.
spring is more than a melting place in the mind
or new kinds of blossom beckoning futures
past your dissolving hands:
perhaps you can forgive the longings for solace
which hurt you so, the brilliant promise of water,
enough to permit a gentleness to wake
the million eyelids sleeping in your skin


\*


Here in riverless Williamstown
cannons pout in the parks. Black swans
pick through mud, scooping crusts
from bags snagged on the rubble. Fish nuzzle
at the outlet from the power station
where water's warm as blood.
Blue jellyfish inflate behind barbed wire.

Once we walked the breakwater,
black basalt laid with ankle bruising stones
broken by convicts. You fell and cried.
I lifted you and carried you, my shoes flayed on the shards,

the hard way back from what you had
imagined - a silver beach
luminous with toyshops, or a ship-shaped cloud:
not, at least, this backwash lapping,
this edgeless sky.

\*

I see frost as if for the first time
when a single frozen dewdrop was enough to entrance me
these days of course I am no longer a child
my skin would run like tears but somehow I must be discrete
love is the self's apocalypse
questioning too deeply as if I had no right to be present there
beneath the dress the feathers beneath the claws a mirror beneath the glass a
      sex of radiant music
beneath the music stars that hurt my eyes
who doesn't want to fly but perhaps it is time to be literal
that infinite trust I used to call a body evaporating in the vivid air
as if the words fall burning down as if the sky shakes free its glorious petals
for that while between whiles
here in the light

# Medea

Forgetting what is mine
as rain sheds its petals
I will show you everything
falling away like water

As rain sheds its petals
in this endless night
falling away like water
from my callussed hands

In this endless night
I think of knives blooming
from my callused hands
and a vast exile

I think of knives blooming
treacherous as lips
and a vast exile
numbs every prayer

Treacherous as lips
curling inside the body's love
numbing every prayer
in blood's filthy clamour

curling inside the body's love
forgetting what is mine
in blood's filthy clamour
I will show you everything

# I will write

I will stop writing and walk out, and in the clamour of commerce I will consider the value of truth.

When I return, the evening light will be yellow and the bird that whistled all day will have fallen silent.

Once again I will discover that I have nothing to say.

Perhaps a bright instrument may flash then, in my empty hands.

# Flames

I have burned my offerings I have counted the omens

I confess my obsolescence freely, I would press my lips to lips which corrode in the high-handed manner of a god

thorn of my soul, why have you covered yourself in blood? what are your legislations?

and who are you, emerging from the waves? a turbulence of money, sight turned redly in, algorithm of lack, ecstatic spasm?

you leave this mask of blue flesh, this burned shoe by a roadside, if there were an answer to be made it shouldn't be to you

but moralising is easy, being fatal, and nothing is easy, not a child's petty greed, nor desire's treachery, my own face my enemy, my feet groundless

I count my days as vanishings, as silences extruded from a poisoned dusk, despairs whisper their names and throttle infancies before my eyes

nothing against such certainties but a hand's shadow raised against extinction, a trivial heat

who follows through this night of ghosts the rumours of another vision?
who dreams these baubles dazzled by a gentler light?

# A digression

Being proved non-existent, I rejoiced in the delicious air. Alas, an angel grabbed me by the heel and started whispering flatteries. I floated to the ground in order to hear him more clearly.

As the dust cleared, I saw the usual disasters were taking place on a huge screen in the city square. A hundred children vanished in a puff of smoke. A magician pushed his goggles onto his forehead and scratched his nose. A woman sang the same words over and over again.

Then I noticed how many people were shopping. They walked indifferently past a man who was weeping on a unicycle. Everything they bought turned to rubbish in their hands.

I realised I must be at a fairy ball and that all those masks were futile defences against enchantment. Only the clown bought nothing. He ground a pomegranate into pulp with his oversize heels but not one coin clattered into his hat.

I thought he must be very joyful, to be weeping so copiously. But as I approached to ask his secret, he turned and vanished into a department store. A beggar started foaming at the mouth and ran down three fat children with a knife and fork. A mangy dog with worms drilling its back was fossicking in a bin.

What is this? I asked the angel. And who dictates these horrors? But the angel was trying on a new tuxedo.

From this level I could see how each smile dissipated into the dust of reflections. Again I demanded, What is this?

An answer came back to me like confetti on a cold wind. It is called the Real World, the angel said.

It doesn't look real to me, I answered, but he had already gone.

# This window

Another day spills over the water
and wastes its magnificence on the blind
flanks of emptying offices,

and is not grateful for the wretched dues
you pay in the sweat you wash away
every night down a dwindling plughole,

the puzzles of a life that slips and vanishes
between a freeway and a darkening room,
halting and jerking like a television

no one bothers to watch, a habitual play
worn white by too many washings
through too many eyes, your protest

not silenced but unnoticed, merely one
of many cries, the real and the imagined,
the lost and the living and the dead.

This window is a frame for the sky
you long to touch, as perplexed as words
that finally are never sufficient,

as if one might look in and see
a glimpse of a pure thing before the glass
crazes over and the room burns.

# Saint

You became a dark earth on the back
of a real sun, which blazed in credulous eyes.
When you shot the lamb, its bleat
festered like a splinter.
At 3am the lights throbbed like veins
on dark men who staggered out of clubs
smelling of starvation.
You knew them all, the shout, the fist, the eyes
like stale urine. You went inside.
A woman lay bound and gagged on a table.
You took out your wounds and laid them beside her.
She kept breathing, staring straight ahead.
At last you remembered the sun, its whiteness,
the clarity of steel.
You left her there, familiar at last, and your hands
smelt of sweet acid. It was dawn again.

# Witchcharm

leave only your absence
        for those moonblind hounds
                they can't snout
shadow from shudder
                velvet from cowpat

      repair to the clean night
              which waits you

        *for sweetness parsley*
        *and marjoram to drive away serpents*
        *and as remedy against the sour & queasy stomach*

hagridden by their own howlings
      they conjure feverish
            phlegm-pale flesh
                biddable to vacancies
        of bridle and bitten
            of cold cunt flayed
on absolute stone

        *st johns wort the most precious remedy*
        *for any wound made*
        *with a venomed weapon*
        *henbane which avails*
        *against all botches*

but you are a lustre
        that predatory eyes
may not comprehend

                      icicle shattering
            to brilliant spectra
    womb of lightnings

        *fragrant simmer*
                *against the rim of speech*
*the bowl and the table*
            *and such lilies*
        *of the seemly and beautiful shape*
        *that is their own virtue*

# Poem for Zoe

love trips on a broken step
and shows me the small moon
hidden in her foot

she gave me the stone
that beats in my pocket
the feather of a crow

some nights the sea wanders inland
and covers the moon
with a nightdress of salt

it may speak of love
as if we can riddle what it means
it passes in like remembering

the body in a small bed
snores as the sea creeps around her
with necklaces of fish and green bones

winter comes and goes
like the breath of a child
ravenously dreaming

# The wind

I am done with everything but this business
of recalling what is human -
faint letterings in sand, this burning leaf
or a curtain blooming in a still room -
all I know of eternity. How it burns me,
how borderless I become in the wind
evaporating like the sweat of fingers
and blown blindly over the blind ocean -
no mark will tell the wind of my presence
my feet will fail to remember you
dancing in a dark room
o my love how the windows shudder

# Money

tonight a small boy is weeping in a forest
he misses the black dog which lay down beside him
if he lives he'll shape his heart around a trigger
        tell it to the birds
           if any are left to sing of it

a man with ambitions sold him down the river
a woman with a microphone identified the price
a beggar on the riverbank knelt down and held him
        tell it to the birds
           if any are left to sing of it

what price a brain smoking in the mud?
what price a baby spitted like a piglet?
what price a cunt ripped open with a rifle?
        tell it to the birds
           if any are left to sing of it

the man in the bunker makes love to his money
the poor woman pulls a pebble from her pocket
and the face of a child rubbed pale as a dream
        tell it to the birds
           if any are left to sing of it

# Language

This of course has nothing to do with words which
may be hammered into atoms or dressed in tulle
whatever you like they will do what you say
obediently, biding their time.
They'll outlast you anyway.

How to bud into this world that makes you so lonely.
How to become pitiless enough
to see one singular thing.
How to murder the god in yourself
in order to discover an absence
you might believe in -
those sorts of questions -

and how the grammar of love
depends on the spaces and
those several others
who continually insist on the sky
and today it really is blue and white
and closer than any language.

# Where are the dark woods?

they were always there
from the beginning
infant eyes open and blink on them

the world as it always was
unredeemed by history
abashing childsight in a whitening room

and other quotidian amputations
flaring distantly now a starry abstraction

inflamed absences
eat the scratched and damaged skin
imagined as soul

who can afford to flinch at pain
the one gate left open?

that memory of complete sufficiency
a dark pulse of heaven

we have already been there and won't go back
astir in the knived light

# Mnemosyne

*the love unseen and the love unheard and the love unsaid: the love in love*
Proem, Octavio Paz

**I**

I didn't want babies I didn't like dolls I poked my fingers into their dumb eyes and drew measles on their faces I hated dresses I walked in the bush and wrote new kinds of flowers I built dams in the backyard I liked making huts with bark roofs I sat inside them and looked out through the window holes I liked banging nails into the wood I liked making cages I liked tightening the wire on fences with a key I never cried when the wire sprang back I had hard feet and walked on gravel I could kill rabbits I could feed baby magpies I could tell the time by the sun when I slashed my fingers I never cried I read books I was clever I could build huts but I never lived in them I went somewhere else I looked at the moon I lay in the grass I didn't know what I wanted but I never wanted babies not ever I never cried

**II**

no eye no fingerprint no nose no lips no voice unnamed unthought unknown un

til

the brain's soft galaxy

unlids itself and sucks the tang of sea

dividing into time

cell by cell by cell

## III

I tried to remember when my sister was born what it was like to be inside my mummy but I could never remember all I got was blank

I pressed my eyes to get all dark the red suns under my fingers opened and closed

I wished I could ask my sister because she was soon enough to remember but she couldn't talk yet and talking meant forgetting

I listened to the waves across my mummy's belly it's the baby she told me and I wondered

I never could remember

**IV**

she writhes into the mystery of her body

herself dissolves and remakes itself

will not be still won't stop it's eating her it's closed her up she's lost inside alone she hurts there are no words there is no hand no tongue no god no hate no love nothing to save her

a crush a must a burn afraid a breath a

# V

does the cell grieve when it splits? does the ovum wince at the sperm?

does the grain cry out as it bursts open? does the laurel scream its leaves of flame?

becoming other becoming one becoming other: the surface tears and heals: a mouth breaks open:

light dazzles off the skin: the eye blinks shut: when it wakes everything is different

## VI

a snake of fire tightens its bones inching the endless tree of you

sweat stinging your eyes blind

the world's waters breaking inside you

time no more there's only now this breath

a sun a red sun

## VII

the first blood came I said nothing I hid myself inside myself I felt me swelling me me me and all myself so different now the front swelled up the hips swelling the fur dark on dark places I saw my mother's fear her death inside me pain my other secret life my joy my shame my joy

## VIII

she delicious as cusped moons as Dante saw the girlwoman radiant on the bridge

tenderbreasted slenderwombed the menses slipping silk between her legs

straightly poised to right the pride of curves her mouth judges a new weight

she moves hieratic and solemnly the generous woman breaking into her face

## IX

bearing past all bearing bearing down
the soft anointed fontanelle of my daughter

shuddered into light the next
beginning

# X

the poem is a womb where the sole cell doubles and doubles and doubles and doubles into a face you cannot recognise

it is an eye which doubles out of your love it grows as far beyond you as the sunlight warming your fingers

you pick it up like a gun and look down the barrel its blue metal flowers into mosquitoes

bees moths butterflies beetles the winged exoskeletal queens circle your head you sneeze and they vanish

they enter your bones they eat their way to your soul the red sun rising inside already isn't you

one day soon the wings will break out of your eyes and then how will you see?

what will your mouth do, flying like that, those two halves of a lost moon?

# Phrases

your mysteries as full as skin I trace them with my cooler fingers

is it your eyelid or your weeping cock each bends its sight to me so tenderly

all ends of you are you and all wet labia singing clear as eyes as liquid glass overrunning itself ah there are mosses and snails beyond the naming of science and unimaginable sunrises and teeth offered up by ingenuous evenings

we are the cake and the candles the breath the tongue and the cup all multiplications and spendings all possible spells

the bestiaries of excess with every fabulous mouth each naked and feathered wing all beaks and talons and scales the monsters breaking these mirrors with their transparent savageries all of them true and hurtled and lathered at last a child's rhyme

breathed out against the dark

# Suttee

I was the sick one in a forest of icicles
I looked out windows and the stone looked back
eating the morning sun as if it were emeralds
everywhere windows and everywhere flowers burning
everywhere viruses sweating out of the earth

I had no time for their careful measurements
already busy with the swift decays
how brittle these arms reach towards the end of things
talking it so comfortable it's frightening
and these glass screens glaring and a music
strange and intimate like the hum of cars
or jets screaming so high you cannot see them
imagining the sky itself is screaming

no might I say to the demon it is spring
and a child leap from my vulva like a coal
flaming and alive and consuming itself
no I might say it is the afternoon of me
these endless flanks of sand and a single
silhouette where once unsalted
an oakapple wove itself to itself
no I might say it was a wound reopening
like the night which deepens in a locked room
a deadly rose seductive and odorous
the red pulse of rain in an empty house
the ghost in the mirror like a cut hand
o lovely lovely violence

whispers the demon the locks are mute
in the planet's hollow children are screaming
they are not my children their lips bleed in my skull
my skin a lace of burns the soft air hurts
yes I would sleep in thy mild arms o black flower I would
sleep and never wake again

# From the West Gate Bridge

    I have forgotten again
           how beautifully this city dreams
              in blue neons and sodium
its silent ships which glide along the black river
              under the red cranes

how ripples of moon die under the bridges
                      only to be born again
        and again against the breakwaters

how the empty freeway
           slickers red and yellow
      over the terminal
and its massiveness seems gentle now

under the spring rain
          which forgives everything
                    with an equal tenderness
    and reveals nothing
but its live lips
          brushing my hair

# I like to think about my beloved

I like to think about my beloved it is
a great pleasure to me she
scatters himself all over my neurones
wearing a set of completely different faces
this amuses me and also how he
walks into lamp posts when I call her
from across the street and the way
noticing the asymmetry of his face makes
my stomach lurch or you know how hands are
so suddenly revealing all that stuff and if
my beloved exists it would be necessary
to make them up unless you find a way of
saying mine that means everything but
me or a way of belonging which can overthrow
capitalism one likes to think that love
might do such a thing but except for that
particular flame which illuminates
beyond the self's penumbra and permits
the real to happen there seems
small hope of that and yes love might be
a lie which calls the truth but first you have to
know which is the lie and usually
people get lost in hallucinations or decide
that love is more important than their beloved
and after all there are so many kinds of love and so
many beloveds and none of them can
breathe in other people's dreams and at the end
of the day I like to think in particulars it is
more erotic and perhaps less deadly

# Once upon a time

He was born inside a nut which grew at the top of the highest tree in the world. The tree grew on an island in the middle of a copper blue lake. One day a blackbird came along and pecked the nutshell with its yellow beak and his eyes split open. He hadn't known there were so many colours. When the blackbird asked him if he wanted to climb onto its back he did, just like that. They flew away from the tree over the blue lake until they came to the other shore. There the blackbird set him down and he looked around. He was bigger than a crocus flower, and that seemed very big to him, but the world was bigger still. He looked at the sky and wondered if he could touch it. He touched the earth and wondered if he could fly through it. He thought the air and the water were the same thing. He didn't know anything. 'What shall I do?' he asked the blackbird. 'I don't know anything.' The blackbird flew away without answering. He sat on a stone on the edge of the lake looking at the blue world. The wind was very cold. Something wet ran down his face, but he didn't know what it was. He started to sing.

# The letters of the good mothers

*(Freely constructed from a letter by Sor Juana de la Cruz)*

the letters of the good mothers
are drenched in secular eloquence
if all the limbs of my body were tongues
I could not publish such excellence

they do not hasten to condemn
deformities of the human heart
yet ambition may become a woman
*muliere in silentio discat*

the properties of a hare may briefly
make a woman handsome
but I would rather ungreased hinges
and the study of declensions

*osculatur me osculo*
*oris sui* decrees the Song
if lips were letters I could more straitly
be given to wondering

for this pure grammar of kisses
may express a pious verity
that mitigates the condemnations
of lascivious sorority

if a harp can cure a king's sickness
then song may heal my sin
I merely lust to follow studies
that are celebrated in men

# Poetry on tv

yesterday I was sick as a dog
        so I took all my drugs and turned on the tv
I don't usually watch tv because I find it too depressing
        all this stuff I am supposed to buy
        and those blow-waved commentators ratcheting up the fear meter
cancer scares life threatening elevators terrorists &c
        but anyway there I was pasted to the sofa
            and I saw two programs with poets in them!
one was all about counter-terrorism in Yemen
        a handsome poet whose name I didn't write down went out
             to tribal villages with his ceremonial knife in his belt
        and in a long room would speak his poems to about forty men
            who would chew mildly narcotic leaves
                while listening to the true way of Islam
            how it is a religion of peace and tolerance
        and how killing people is not Islamic
this poet was a former army officer but was now a man of peace
        and he was greatly honoured among the villagers
then I got embarrassed because the Australian journalist
        was interviewing some boys in an Islamic school in Yemen
                and all he would talk about was Al Qaeda
            so I switched and there was a program about The Last Poets
            and how poetry was about Revolution
                and Black Power and how poetry
        saved at least one person's life
because it stopped this guy when he was about to drive a knife
            into another person's heart because he was a gangster

  then they talked about rap and money
      and how the whole thing had got corrupt
           and I began to feel depressed again
       because in both of these programs there was not one woman
        mentioned or spoken to
    and nobody seemed to think this was strange
  or worth talking about

# Thoreau in Chernobyl

The woods were beautiful as always, but dry.
It seemed a subtle poison at the roots
drained them imperceptibly of life.
A want, or heightened colour, in each leaf
hinted profound disease, as if the rites
of generation faltered and withdrew
beyond emergencies of flood and fire
to deserts that no green could penetrate.
I shaped my stanzas, but the form seemed trite:
all metre euphemised a deepening flaw.
I heard no frog calls, and the birds were fewer
in species and in number. I trod
ungodly glows, a covenant betrayed,
a humus rotting slowly into fear.

# Persephone

a bad season
veins death silted
seeped through skin
wrecking her sight
counted his riches
his lackeys filing
smuggled for ripeness
cocaine coffee
so many shapes

all that winter
toxic liquids
rainbow glamour
as the underking
*mine or nothing*
cargos of lust
bonded muscles
cash & weapons
so many dollars

she squats in the dark
letting the death out
him in his suit
blind as a razor
she wonders aloud
heaps in the mind
touch to possess
of what is itself
small & mean
that can't bought
is nevertheless
not-you not-yours

opens her veins
*o the banality*
pure & impeccable
can gods be fake?
is it that money
how those hands
hating the scent
a gun's blank mouth
takes care of things
or bribed or what
the floating free

*nothing*

you vain whore
why d'you think
take yr famine
take yr tears
think it matters?

he said at the gate
it's all about you
out of my house
yr tedious murder
I can buy virtue

this is my house
my dogs are by
will rip you up
if that's what you want
there's richer earth
harder stones
there's bigger wheels

spring is dead
in the dark months
letting the death out
*it's too late now*
already eats us
to burn up africa
the desert continent
on sacred mountain
where forests were
all that was tender
all the uncostable
to friable tinder
the price of that gold
sterile as wheat
you got it all

these my riches
their diamond teeth
and eat yr sex
your whinging's over
than your poor humus
and brighter suns
than your dumb seasons

she said aloud
veins slit open
fuck you hades
you know the sky
summer is coming
summer will pale
dry the four rivers
ash & ember
you won your point
all the unmeasurable
shrunk and withered
waiting for summer
in your underkingdom
in its mutant acres
you got what you paid for

# In the hour of dogs

in the hour of dogs
every human voice
is hushed

night is our scavenge
us and the watchboots
no stranger dares

we prowl as kings
we are the claws and noses
we are the grip

that stalks on stiff legs
rotting ribs and vertebrae
and hostile ankles

the steam of our piss
rises past the towers
and dims stars

# The virgin bride

The virgin bride sleeps dully on her throne,
atrocity a blue scum on her eyelids.
Small boys scrawl obscene cartoons
or pause in their quarrels, hearing the sky
clap open above them, before they return
with greater ferocity. Certainty breasts the horizon
with a cargo of skulls, high on its bridge
a flag of surgical hygiene, and everywhere a dim
splashing as hands are washed
in military-grade disinfectant. The mortar
of civilisation was always the blood in the keystone.
Timur's descendents scanned the skies
with instruments of torture; freedom was bought
with the bourgeoisie's guillotine; beneath
the Doge's gilded maps were layers of stone cells
with iron doors impenetrable as the faces
of informers. The voices beneath history
shriek to the burning heavens
their inconsolable anguish.
Soon a noble moral will be drawn
out of the entrails of children.

# Euterpe

The lamp remains on the table
In its predatory circle of light
Dust rains down on an open book

The suburbs ebb into darkness
Hungry and desolate under antennae
Rats hunt in the weeds

You thought it was beauty
That shocked you to a husk
All your life a collusion with dying

Even the air tastes bitter
Her skeletal wings slice the walls
She lands and opens her eyes

# Mayakovsky

I thought the world was bigger than a bucket
I rhymed potatoes with feathers and lightning
The new meanings blazed like life in a new colour
I rhymed everything with everything

In America I was a genius
That was even better than being famous
I stood on Brooklyn Bridge like a stupid artist
I watched the shivering jobless drown

Meyerhold admired my Mexican carpets
He invented sciences to stage my words
Laughter was our consolation and our weapon
So we rhymed bureaucrat with numbskull

In France I bought a car and a tin of soap
I fell in love and chivvied my longing home
I scrubbed so hard but bedbugs kept on biting
Critics and officials with their insect jaws

There were not enough bath houses not enough soap
My soul itched until it was red meat.
What's left behind when you stand on life's furthest rim?
A scrapbook adding up to nothing

I saw the world was smaller than an orange
I rhymed my body with love and found coffins
The old meanings jumped up like death in a new suit
And then everything rhymed with nothing

# Words

*After Vladimir Mayakovsky*

I know the power of words. I hear their sirens.
They don't pimp applause from expensive seats.
They quicken the weight of things, so coffins burst
Out of the sucking earth, marching on oaken legs.
They might be dumped - unpublished, unprinted -
But words tighten their girths and gallop on anyway.
Centuries crowd around them, trains crawl near
To lick the blistered hands of poetry.
I know the power of words. They float down
Light as petals under a dancer's heels,
But words are the soul meat. Lips and bones.

# A History of Rain

I marvelled at the squid's mantel,
The sloth's curled hook,
The magenta lips of orchids.


Behind me barbed feathers
Tore air to turbulence
And then were still.


The soluble sky thickened
As grief heats an eye
To astonished blindness.


\*

You who love me best,
      Have you traced my pulse
           Through city walls?


I was lost already, I retched
      As oil plumed through my blood.


The clouds are still falling
      Huge and angry wounds.

Your heart is an executive
                Who remembers nothing.
My face is the face of a man
          Who looks down amazed
                      At the murdered thing


\*


It will not lack colour –
consider the intricate brachiation of silica,
pale spicules green with cyanide algae –
conifer needles in snow, their colours
unaccountably reversed –
or the butterfly lustre of sulphur lakes.

Will your eyes blur at this beauty
so unlike you? No, you have long dissolved,
you, your reflections, your aqueous desires,
into the flame-coloured sky.

# To break a silence

to break a silence may be fatal
        or at least injurious
but equally might startle a bower of wings
            out of shaded interiors
the problem is to know what kind of silence
        it may for instance be the quiet
of dusk when minds turn
        inward to the animal that whickers
starwards wonderingly and settles
            on loins of poetry
                licking its teeth
or the wordlessness of the weary
        who study full stops becoming
what they are and who dig their
            dreams into the past having
       already looted the future
                and found there no sweetness
or perhaps a vacancy that might be love or disgust
       but is the reverse of resignation
           although it may sound similar
when dogs shout their evening greetings
                through the purple suburbs
or it might be simply the indifference that masks
      a loathing for inexactitude
a jeweller's morality in which all petty speech
          withers in shame
most perilous of all the silence
        of a stern surface shining so blindingly
           it frightens off words
       with their own distorted reflections
but which breaks when it breaks
          like glass in the raw flesh beneath it

# Specula

**Visions of the world's surface**

*First Vision*

tv antennae rake carnivorous angels dislocate the heart chimes the clock measures sarcomas bulge the flickering heads of saints nothing more alive than this moment

*Second Vision*

I have savaged my skin I have slept in the shadows of rotting architectures eyes backward in my head I see deep into hell I divine the salt taste squamous on my lips I pluck the neon fruits germinating over this lying city I hold myself regretless and yet my hands punish me bristle in the tarmac to splinter my ramparts I flew into the nucleus of the sun and fumigants await me with their cheap smiles earth old and full of her rebellion her seeds swell under fingernails I am florescent again the rose of leprosaria

*Third Vision*

heart bends the weight of everything I have forgotten lingering in the stink of God's breath my deathly Father walking where I am forbidden and birds speak to me darkly I am the black blood breaking under the scourge I write this only because I am told flame bursts over the page how many chimneys have called how many bones how many pyres consumed how many voices I am not these words I am nothing I am not I am a name

*Fourth Vision*

because I am the axeman skulks in the sad carolling of foreign birds I was not the death of myself so much as the agony of beginning

*Fifth Vision*

behold how light splices the frost and trees collect themselves saints depart from their niches childsight vanishes I have slept in my stench faint as an echo on the skin of night

*Sixth Vision*

the owl springs out of my mind she has abandoned me wakes between the night and incurable hurts extrudes huge wings and twilight is impassible my senses vanish I am the sweetness left by god in the inimitable desert where stones never weep all beginnings and all endings whoever waits has no face and I am lost I have been mortal once again there is nothing to save me

## Of Margery of Kempe I

*[T]he husband is his wife's head, to rule her, correct her (if she strays) and restrain her (so she does not fall headlong). For hers is a slippery and weak sex, not to be trusted too easily. Wanton woman is slippery like a snake and mobile as an eel; so she can hardly be guarded or kept within bounds. Some things are so bare that there is nothing by which to get hold of them. . . . so it is with woman: roving and lecherous once she has been stirred by the devil's hoe.*

THIS CREATURE                         where thorw she lost reson and her wyttes
        a long tym
             setting all
hyr trost, alle hyr lofe, and alle hyr affeccyon in hym only
                      he comawnded hyr and charged hir
that sche shuld wryten her **felyngys**
                           *the creature* cryed often

[his eyn myssed so that he mygth not see
         to make hys [hyr] lettre he set
                a peyr of spectacles on hys nose]

**ANNO DOMINE 1436**

[*and then yet it was wretyn fyrst be a man whech cows neithyr wel wryten*]

she had a thyng in conscyens whech sche had nevyr schewyd

THIS CREATURE
went owt of hir mende
                        she knew no vertu ne goodnesse

                                thereof

sche bot hir owen hand so vyolently
                 and also sche roof her skin       wyth her nayles spetowsly

THAN
syttyng upon her beddys syde **lokying** upon hir
                                **how the eye openyd**
as brygth as ony levyn and he stey up into the eyr     fayr and esly
    *that sche mygth wel beholdyn hym in the eyr til it was closyd ageyn*

**Of Life's Mys(t)eries**

*no wound so deep as the mind*

                    sweat
        through menstrual stains to the brittle

skins of
        **I**
    it cracks they is
            dry as dead
    paper              husks

you write
      down
          atrocity
   you write up
                  you mouth
     the bad taste blood you
# SAY
                    the shattered
          skeleton the ripped
       vagina the
burned bone the rotting brain the gashed slitted cracked slashed

      evidence

             of wrong sex
                                             wronged
                  so many words
said    uttered    lipped
                                                    fleshening circles of
                        being and

**yet**

           in the cockeyed courtroom amid the testements these
                         un-words
                         have HAVE BEEN HAD
                have fallen like soft petals sweet
                              candied rosepetals decorative as grief as
        swallowable as tears as liminal as any
                                           metaphor
howlscriesbellowsululationsgroanswailsshrieksroarsbaysyelpssobsscreams
         keening        lamentations        break
                  lips red lips rot lips red
hands red breasts blue nails black teeth how digestible how they oil the
     economies remain  in   visible   hole   absent   sweetnothings
             you

# cunts

## Of Margery of Kempe II

[sche wold not leevyn hir pride ne hir pompows aray
gold pypys on hir hevyd

**alle hir desyr was for to be worshepd of the pepul**

and was on of the grettest brewers in the town
the ale was lost]

*summe seyden sche was acursyd*

### WERE WROTH WITH HIR

*sche herd a sownd of melodye so swet and delectable*

the dette of matrimony was so abhomiably to hir that sche had levar
etyn and dryken the mukke in the chanel
punschyn and chastysyn hemself wylfully be absteyning

*he used her as he had do before*
he wold not spar

*Having once tasted the spirit, she held as nothing all sensual delights until one day she remembered the time when she had been gravely ill and had been forced, from necessity, to eat meat and drink a little wine*

                              he leyd beforn *this creatur*
the snar of letchery and in al this tyme sche had no lust to comown wyth her husbond           in the second year yt fel so that a man whech sche       lovyd wel seyd onto her    he wold ly be hir
and have hys lust of hys body        and sche schuld not withstand him     and evyr sche was labowred wyth the other man for to syn wyth hym        sche was ovrycoym    and consentyd in her mend
and he seyd he ne wold
                       *schamyd and confusyd in hirself*

**boldly clepe me Jhesus thi love for I am thi love and schal be thi love**
                                                                  **wythowtyn ende**

*this creature*
                  hir dalyawns was so swet that sche
gret plenté of terys     boystows sobbyngys     mornyggys and wepyngys

# unspekable

# The Unknown Language

| ENGLISH | LATIN | LINGUA IGNOTA |
|---|---|---|
| Man | Homo | Whose |
| God | Deus | Mouth |
| Sin | Labia | Kisses |
| Angel | Angelus | Wholly |
| Language | Hymen | Without |
| Reason | Logos | Fear |
| Rationality | Ratio | Is |
| Trinity | Uno | Luminous |
| Lust | Desiderio | Delight |
| Devil | Diabolo | Laughing |
| Ignorance | Defututa | Through |
| Master | Magister | Darkly |
| Nature | Natura | Wounded |
| Faith | Fidelis | Flesh |

## Of Margery of Kempe III

*In vehemence of spirit, almost as if she were inebriated, she began to loathe her body when she compared it to the sweetness of the Paschal Lamb and, with a knife, in error cut out a large piece of her flesh which, from embarrassment, she buried in the earth. Inflamed as she was, however, by the intense fire of love, she did not feel the pain of her wound*

                                              **the prest**

**whech wrot this boke**

    thei were ryche men, worshepful marchawntys and haddyn gold enow
            (whech may spede in every nede)   **rewth that mede**

**schuld spede**

                                        **er than trewth**

        **God has nowhere to put his goodness, if not in me**

**thei wer most displeysyd**

                they cutted her gown so schort that it come but lytil
                sche schuld ben holdyn a fool

**ther is no gyft as holy as the gyft of lofe**

and sumtyme yf sche sey a man had a wownde er a best whethyr it wer
    er yyf a man bett a childe befor hir
        er smet a hors er another best wyth a whippe

**hir thowt sche saw owyr Lord be betyn er wowndyd**

                                       lyk as sche saw in the man er in the best

*this creature*

         summe seyd it was a wikkyd spiryt      sum seyd it was a sekenes

             sum seyd sche had dronken to mech wyn

             sum wuld she ben in the se in a bottumless

more ful of wowndys than evyr was duffehows of holys        wondyrfully turnyng and wrestyng her body

                               **alas, alas for sorwe**

      sche wept            sche sobbyd      sche cryed so lowde

*summe seyden that thei wold not go wyth hir for an hundryd pound*

       **the cawse of hys malyce was for sche would not obeyn him**

*my derworthy dowtyr I schal nevyr forsakyn the*

        and yyf sche sey a semly man sche had gret peyn to lokyn on hym

                **the manhode of Crist**

# Dance of the Seven Veils

**FIRST** she is humble and unworthy
         she dare not
              she is diseased
her eyes dilate her fingers bleed her mouth simmers with juice
        she cannot
contain herself she spills
            modestly into the word
       contingent as a virus
             in the corpse of god


**SECOND**  she locks her mouth
    fast on the mouth of a man
           his pen rivers her blood
over the margins
        of god's book


**THIRD**  she is an ear
wet with song she is a cunt swollen
    with god's glory she is an eye
blistered with light she is skin
         split by goading kisses she
      is a stomach parched
   to ecstasies she rakes off
         her hair she is
the pure sex tolling
        through cavities of blood

**FOURTH**    she understands
     how walls melt
          in desire's conflagration


**FIFTH** she sees her lover
    perfected in death
rising to take her
         perfectly unbodied
     kiss
   in his bloodied mouth
his dessicated skin
         pearls and floods
     with the salty waters
          of her many tongues


**SIXTH** she is cast
        into her freedom
   her voice infects
the cloistered ear
          her tumescence
     returns she sleeps
         slimed with sweat her tears
      o'erspill the nightmare chalice
   her lips rot her hands blaze with putrefaction her stink
         fills the chapel with penitents
     she is all parasite ingesting her own juices

        her belly bloats and ulcers
                with the fruit of god

she cries love
      in the crowded streets
   she is untouchable


**SEVENTH**   she burns
             on the pyre built
             letter on letter
             by god's faithful servants


      her blood boils
      her eyeballs burst
      her bones crack and char


      naked
      at last
      in god's great darkness

## Of Margery of Kempe IV

> *Ah! Lord God! Who has written this book? I in*
> *my weakness have written it, because I dared not*
> *hide the gift that is in it.*

sche nevyr tellyn how swet it wern                        many white thyngys

         sweche sowndys and melodiis      the fyer of love brennyng
             voys of a lityl bird that song ful merily

thu schalt heryn that thu nevyr herdist         thu schalt felyn
               thu plesyn me so wel
                           I am alwey plesyd with the

thu mayest boldly when thu art in thi bed
            take me to the as thi wedded husbond
                      ——as thi derworthy derlyng and thu
mayest
boldly        kyssen my mowth
                  my lofe is evyr redy to the
ne thu can han no other comfort but me only
         whech am I
           thi God
               and am al joy and al blysse to the

# The Kingdom

no the kingdom is not yet
                laboured out of flame
                and many the heads broken
against its borders
        beyond hope of healing


all confusion and clamour
                buying and selling
                icons and pretty stories
words prepare our injuries
        and keep us from them


and slice now to its pith
                a fiery desolation
                raining from heaven
deathrut in the ancient ways
        prosecutes in each again


men blister ripe on the wartree
                and women splay
                for maggot pleasures
uniforms of bone and gristle
        haft their weapons


scouring every storied skull
                the limed charnel
                stinks with life
which goes about its business
        eating and burning

   they say the kingdom is not visible
                      all circles must be broken
                 inside or outside
it shines beyond all conflict it is the agony
         some say that it will never come

# O my america

I

o the ice pick sings
        its hot orange
                in the vendetta tree
     such tales for telling
through these numb fingers
             one by one


rubies such as never seen
        in the caught months
             of a fatal spring
                    sad & toxic

II

my dear america
             the uranium sun
      coals on your many tongues
                unjust and bleeding


all these broken songs
       out of the trap
             beads weapons money
                turn & snap

                    which skull split
        in the berth of which paroxysmal
                        vision of which
                                oily hell


                    a whale of a time
        america you clamp your arrogant jaw
                            down again that
                                    beautiful machine
                breaks breaks again breaks

# If in foregone times

If in foregone times master smiths tempered a blade, folding and refolding steel to its most piquant edge, so in this we have perfected the technologies of harm. The chronicles claim that as we have become subtle in inflicting pain, balancing the maximum of consciousness and the maximum of agony to a point finer than a micron, so we are now coarsened in our joys. This protest betrays an indefensible nostalgia, the birthing of a memory which in turn labours into imagination. Imagination, the chronicles claim, is the single cell which metastasises into love. The sages are too wise not to perceive the transparency of their prophecies, but nevertheless continue to believe them.

*

In any case, who can hunt meaning through these thickets? Too much is imperfectly understood to leave a clean scent. Traces resolve as the simulacra of too many selves, vanishing as the yelping packs pursue them. Desire is both subtle and coarse: too evasive for our crude instruments and yet so predictable in its instincts. In unguarded moments I found myself longing for the dazzling conceits of civilisation to be actual, for the profound and bloody pleasures which underlay them. I was trapped in a softly lit room while darkness drew its mantle of cries into the range of hearing. Such shy animals as love, naturally, remained beyond even the cries.

# There are breakages certainly

there are breakages certainly

although bone can withstand more pressure than reinforced concrete

the psyche has its own architectures which pay little heed to gravity

an entire city can be populated on foundations little bigger than an ant

I have often watched these insects crawling across the desolations of tables

in such malarial humidities perception is closed to a perimeter of twenty feet

the night is making jaguar roars to scare away the blue skinned animals

within the circle of sight all objects are pretenaturally large and clear

I sip again the vitreous humours of my companions

and I have detached each lunate from each wrist and woven a palace from each

the dust from the ulysses butterfly is an excellent material for windows

such altitudes are dizzying but easily dispersed in alcohol

later the body will wither and every palace crash to the earth

# Why I Am Not A Scientist

I have never been the least use at mathematics.
I sometimes worry about it.
Which part of my brain doesn't add up?
How can I attain equanimity?
What will calculate my multiplicities and divisions?

I was a disturbed and angry child.
Once I scored zero in a test
for organic chemistry.
When my teacher read my mark out
in front of the class to shame me
I stared at him without blinking
to show that I didn't care.

The thing was that I didn't care
but I still wanted him to know
that it was him who was small
not me.

Maybe if I had ever got a handle on maths
I could have measured things better.
In any case that was the end of my ambition
to be a veterinarian.
I can't really blame that chemistry teacher
for the fact that I never could do organic equations
or for the poetry
but sometimes it's tempting.

# Bees

the bees have declared an amnesty
their dances are only lyrical effusions

and why are apricots so illiterate?
yet they diffuse their promiscuous perfumes
sliming the earth with rot

one has always mistrusted the language of cats
and their devotion to hygiene

so many things slide and tumble
churches flounder in tides of mud
shoes dissolve in a week

and why do scissors keep disappearing?
if you ask nature for absolution
it senselessly posts you flowers and blood

and fronds uncurl to tinier fronds and so on
which seem meticulous synonyms for murder

like a froth of hands on metallic surfaces
making and unmaking
and underneath the mindless carnivorous ocean

# Couplets

the irises are plundered
from the king's empty garden

a child draws a circle
in the mud

\*

remember you are unwelcome
and the door is shut

a radio plays Bach
in another room

like a dream of presence
long ago

\*

absolute poem
mocks the empty hand

divides itself by infinity
resolves as nothing

\*

everything that is said
everything that is not said

the jar of tears
by the door of the theatre

where tiny fish
swim like words of light

\*

in the raw wash of dawn
birds assert their territories

their cursive flight
a plain fact of survival

\*

no one is waiting
at that blank address

no one wishes for your presence
no one will welcome you

the sunlight in that room
tastes of dust

\*

where shall I place my lament?
the heart is deaf

the stars have vanished
entirely

\*

no one set the violet
in these rocks

the desert hunters
planted nothing

but the raw bone
of their song

\*

there was a pool that solaced you
in the middle of the forest

in the middle of the pool
was a green eye

it looked straight into the sun
it never blinked

\*

my soul thirsts, o beloved rain
listening for your steps

I will lie down
in the rumour of your undressing

to whisper in your humours
all night long

\*

but when you open the door
you will find the irises on the table

gathering night in their petals
just as you dreamed

# Alley

Infatuation goes unnoticed.
        Within the body's ills
                Evening turns to metaphor.
        The street is unusually empty.
Every weather shines.

A name is more than waiting.
        All silences collude.
                The slaughterhouse of the psyche
        Rattles its hooks.
The mood is blood.

An unidentified shape
        Blooms in the nightwatch
                Ambiguous as a stamen.
        A face full of fist
Gathering up the light.

# Schwittering

my darling o you dahlia
of my third eye teased and pinked for
that enormous sneeze if I had any serious tigers
they'd growl and purl for you like butter
pumpkins fattening in their patches they'd be smiles wider
than water wheels or baobabs and if I
had my way it would be out of here straight past starship
enterprise to mistress joy and all
her deadly pulsars yes you mix me up and down and out
I go trala my fingers trailing fragrant
flocks of meteors or silky bolts
brighter than entire skies but each of me so animal
we curl into your palm with every pore
a pout until the universe unpicks its seams
and lets all its impossibles

# Theatre

predictable as a tragedy
        leached of all colours
in which the painted actress
                pouts and blinks


such blackening tears that all defences choke
        on the absurd
ancient seductions
                smashing the heart


again    finally
        in this yellow dusk she understands
how action breached before its time
                might be fatal


how innocence might summon
        a  dazzling mirage
populous and exact in every detail
                while the desert breathes


livingly beneath it
        cheated of the eye
she asks    which is more real
                the love that gathers


out of our delusions
        in all its tender
quickness of flesh    or the blind
                desiring cell

the torment is always     as the woman said
            to find oneself speaking
like a bad novel   though fiction is seldom
                              so misleading


as these selves we claim
            to live by     squatting
by middens of bone that the wind
                              scours to whiteness


et cetera     she asks:
            if I have been asleep
how does the anguish of dream
                              differ from waking


and is this really my own damage
            or a wound torn in others
that they must diagnose
                              through my skin?

# Goodnight, sweet prince

Such possessions as gore me pontificate from corners.
I am no longer solid but a speech of butterflies.
How it spills, when all is said and done:
It is hard to see virtue in the cold matter
Staining the floor - frills, cups, leaves, arquebuses,
Bile - the gross litters of meaning - the new king
Knitting up this mess in his brainless sinews,
Mere presence the answer to everything, the golden
Halo of a new dawn impressing all the peasants.

# Iseult

I am a queen at a high window
a black sail stands
at exactly the same distance
as always
which means the opposite
of whatever I take it to mean
I can't speak
no matter how many words
clot on the cold floor
here the weather is harsh
and full of dust
words cut me as usual
or the usual words cut me
or was it someone else
some nursery rhymes are deadly
all of them are cruel
I can't stitch a meaning
it unpicks itself
night after night
when so many impediments
swell my tongue
you are the bitterest
heavier than rings or water
colder than a flock of birds
dispersed by storm
there is no true north

the stars oscillate

in unfamiliar orbits

the earth is strange

and marvellous

as winter is

and now is further away

than ever

# Possible Elegies

**1**

There's never been an excuse, you always knew
it was easier to ignore, to drown this hollowing voice
in cascades of inertia. Their fluid columns
fall with a certain beauty after all, and smash
stunningly into your stillness, as if there really were
something happening, as if those tossed reflections
were faces that belonged to you. And what of the recessed
demons who grin and turn away, the flames
are flickering darkly against the roof of your mouth.
It takes so long to be obvious. If you knew who to call
your throat would be full of god, but the code slips past you,
and you just wait on the train between stations,
watching the sky break open and float away.
Behind the afternoon are stars that only the darkness can beckon,
behind those faces a flame is waiting for nightfall,
impossible bridges arc over the horizons
in inexplicable colours, as if a dream came real
and stepped outside you, and all this beauty were yours.

You watch your hand on the cliff face, it seems astounding
such power could curl inside it, to lift a bottle of lye
or drive a knife through skin or sign the ultimatum,
one small act and everything is different. What world is this
that has such choices in it? Yet when the ads peel back
their dazzling skins, who cares? That late-night horror
plays again and again, the blood-mouthed woman
stretches out on the shiny car, the planet goes on dying

under the welts of a billion poverties, and all the little flies
curl up and buzz inside a billion webs. Their prismed wings
are clogged with dust, and at this distance panic
dulls to a drowsy hum. Who were you waiting for? Angels?
Or have they abandoned the earth, being abandoned?

As if the tight white ball of a bud on an orange tree
could save you, as if the rose-coloured light
that alters a street of naked trees were a blessing,
you wait, trusting the warped seasons. You hear
that the art of hope is obsolete, and wipe your benchtops
clean with poison, turn on the silent clocks, measure
your life with whitegoods. And who now stalks these cavities,
monstrous with belief? Was it a god, were those plutonium wings
once made of feathers? It's not as if you can see
the path of its voice, the dread scorching beneath your skin.
It's not as if you know why your hair stiffens
with awe. And is there anything bigger than you, that galaxy
afloat in your skull? Where to begin?

**2**

I understand the desolation of flowers.
My companion, your hands are cruel lilies
grasping for life, whispering of ash and bones –
my companion, even you cannot touch my isolation.
Smoke darkens the sky, a planet of fires
where each of us warms our bodies, the sky is a crematorium
that we cannot see with our eyes, although we feel it in every cell
where the bitter salt is rising.

Even in this quiet hour, I can remember the tumult.
It was the colour of lips, it was the shape of sunset.
When birds flew out of the earth, I caught them in my hungry skin,
their shrill cries were my challenge and my desire.
How many wounds have mounted to this sorrow?

And when you wake, the winds are too high, we are too good at breaking.
How will you count the leaves that no longer exist?
What will you say when the possible languages fail?
How carelessly we move through catastrophe,
our eyes fixed on a horizon that will never behold us.
Creatures fade because they cannot live with so many walls,
already my childhood shines with the remoteness of myth
and I believe those voices who shill for my penitence
no more than men who live in canyons of glass
making bombs with the names of women and flowers.
O the deadly lie of salvation. Beyond their grasp

are the strict parabolas of joy, a faith that leaps
from finger to finger, as real as the hand that holds this pen,
that pulses in sunlight and shadow, a warmth on the darkening earth,
that one day will be gone, memory, smoke, not even that.
Who will you touch, my hand, when you are nothing?

**3**

Sometimes the light is too big for you, it floods your retina
with unbearable radiance, and you push shut your eyelids
as if you were afraid, your sight scorched
by the edges of things, the stylus cut
between one word and another, marking a line
where this is no longer that, where chairs
stand clean in the evening light, and on the table
the knife, the salt, the bottle lie in their terrible separateness,
undissolved by flux, unmoving. How generous is the air
that connects these things, edge to edge, invisible flood
warmed in the lamp of my chest? I breathe
and everything shifts, I breathe and all this sharpness blurs
so nothing is as it was or will be, I breathe and fear transforms
into the feathered present, one of countless things
gifted as texture – the harmonica my son is blowing
in the next room, the heaviness in my shoulders, the dog's grunting
search for fleas, the mortal sunlight glancing through leaves –
Somewhere else a bomb is killing a child. Somewhere else
grief congeals the sky like a plume of smoke
mounting out of a smashed building. Somewhere else
edges are shifted to stranger borders, the moment between
one heartbeat and the splinter that stills it. Even this
is merely a demonstration, price no object, of how a line
must be drawn and drawn again, lest the breath
that warms an orange, say, or the skin of a child
might mist the borders, warming eyes with recognition,
might sing across a wall or through a window

to an uncertain ear, might make the letters of law
shimmer from stone and dance. Who would believe then
those syllables of righteousness, falling from the lips of liars?
Who would want to kill, when orange is so sweet on the tongue,
when the day is to and fro, like the smell of laundry in springtime
giddying nonsense with the wind, and desire rises
softly from the pit of the belly, tender and inconsequential,
fluid as the touch of laughter? The curves of women
must always be despised, the mouth that whispers
hope must welter in blood, the rubble collapse
across a field sown with teeth, nourishing dragons that rise
real and absolute, blasting love to cinders, so its complex pollen
will never drift again in those blistered orchards.
The phosphorous light boils dry the aqueous glow of eyes,
the light strips the possible skin, the light erases everything
but the line between one thing and another. That line is built of words
tangled with barbed wire, bristling with sentries.
No one must get in. No one must get out. The righteous
draw their lines, deep in their bunkers, where the infinite shapes of pollen
are filtered out of the dry air, and there are no shadows.

**4**

And where are you now, my soul? Didn't I glimpse you
in some fluorescent corridor, a ghost in the glass
hurrying through a dim afternoon, your face
composed like a mask? It seemed you were thinking
of something beyond the brief you held to your breast, but knew
that words must be dealt with, before you turned
to the pain that quivers inside you, the quick light
rising like salt, seductive and toxic, that at last you know
is the price of all your days. I wanted to tell you to stay, I wanted
to take your hand and feel its hot grief blazing up
my vanishing arm, until my vision dazzled
like rain in winter sunlight. But perhaps it wasn't you.

# On lyric

*Must I not begin to trust somewhere?*
- Wittgenstein, On Certainty

1

The poet asserts

2

a poet has no responsibility to what has already been said because what the poet says has not been said before

the poet says what has never been said because no moment is time is the same as any other moment in time

the eternal is the present

and so the present moves beyond particularity

the poem is made of language which is made of the human past of individual and collective memory

nevertheless to ask whether a poem is universal is to ask the wrong question

a poem can either enter another present which differs from the present in which it is written or it cannot a poem may be able to inhabit the present of a single individual at one time but not at another or may not enter the present of an individual at any time or may enter at any time

when it enters another present the poem is transformed because no moment in time is the same as any other moment in time

a poem is eternal only in this sense and only in its ceaseless transformation

it is particular to any of the presents involved and in the complexities of the particularities of the presents is not susceptible to the conceptual reductiveness of laws

to ask of a poem that it obey a law is to desire that its freedom is circumscribed

it is to ask it not to be a poem


3


a poem is not a mirror but a breath in the world the world is inhaled translated and exhaled

a poem is not a representation but a mimicry of relationships in the world it is in motion as a gesture is

lyric is not a category but a dimension of a poem

lyric might be thought of as the field of force of a poem

the conditions of its occurrence are potentially infinite

the freedom of the present of a poem is inverse to the extent to which the lyric dimension is eschewed

**4**

lyric is the desire towards the invisibility of the self

the dilemma of encountering lyric is to accept invisibility without shame

the dispossessed, the marginalised and the powerless are invisible

to be invisible is to be without purchase

the self the facets of which are fixed by the shifting gaze of others is endangered it is necessary to protect our visibility in order to have a self with which to move through the world

in being that self we are not free we are constrained by the gaze of others

if we escape the gaze of others we can permit more fully the potential of what is constrained by the creation of a self

what is most constrained is the world we understand by feeling

the desire for invisibility is a desire towards the truth of feeling

invisibility is a gamble on the hope of true habitation in the world

**5**

touch is the seed of feeling

the sense of touch is the root sense by which we know ourselves in the world

the light which touches our retina invokes sight the soundwaves moving through air touch the instruments of our ears the molecules of matter touch us into taste and smell

touch is the first thing we know and the last thing we know

it is the beginning and end of aesthetic and the beginning and end of our humanity

the poet is blind not in order to see but to feel

lyric is the poetry of touch

the vibrations of sound on the organs of the ear translate the imagined distance of worded image into the intimacy of touch

we respond to those vibrations even in the imaginary silence of reading

when we are touched by lyric we wake to the intolerable beauty of our world

6

lyric is a metaphor for feeling

the truth of lyric is particular to each poem and resides in the accuracy of its relationship to feeling

this truth may only be evaluated in the present in which lyric is encountered

it impossible to predict or control

feeling is our vibrational responses to our relatednesses to our world it is as incorrigible as pain and encompasses the totality of our responses moment to moment

it is the consequence of the corporeality of each of us and as complex and mortal as our corporeality

a poem seeks to inhabit our corporeality but knows it cannot express it

7

lyric is indefensible

it neither seeks nor answers an argument but exists in the vibrationary exchange of feeling

the incorrigibility of feeling within lyric breathes unease into all totalities

even if all a person's thoughts were legible to another that other would still not understand the felt world of that person

the felt world of that person is secret

lyric does not disclose its secret its secret is enclosed and retreats as lyric is interrogated it exists as a resonance which may resonate in the present in which it is read or heard

a poem may not be paraphrased or explained it may only be read again

it is the dimension of lyric which cannot be paraphrased

its meanings reside acutely in the relationships of the parts of lyric each to each other

lyric is the same question as 'I am'

lyric is neither rational nor irrational as the rational has no ability to explain the incorrigibility of feeling

feeling is not irrational although its consequences are sometimes expressed in irrationalities

it has this in common with reason: that reason is forever without ground

8

the I of a lyric is neither a self nor a not-self

the I is lyric's protection against totalities for the I is aware of its incompletion the illusion of the totality of the self was always a misunderstanding

it is the mistake of those made uneasy by the lyric's assertion of feeling

the I is what a person makes when translated into feeling which is released from the constraints of exterior gaze

lyric is made when that feeling is translated into language

the relationship of words within lyric are the means by which it mimics the reality of feeling, which is how we know our relatedness to the world

the translations of lyric are always made in the humility of approximation

the metaphor is the most precise means of approximation

to unite two different things in one metaphor is to make a third thing which is at once neither and both of those things

a metaphor can resonate across probabilities in a directed way which mitigates the self's control in either the writer or the reader

each lyric has negations which are particular to itself

a lyric's negation is simultaneously an assertion

the existence of what is negated is felt in the present of the one whom lyric's presence inhabits

the gaps or the silences in the lyric are as important as the words

they notate the relationships between the words and indicate the lyric's relationship to reality

reality is what always lies beyond the lyric

it is the corporeality of the people who encounter the poem and the details of their relationships to their worlds

reality is what the lyric encounters when it enters the present of another person in another time or when it emerges in the present of the poet

the reality of a particular poem is always changing

lyric is not reality

it is real

## 9

lyric is the eroticism of language

the consciousness of lyric is the consciousness of love

in lyric the subject and object relate equally

the subject is a consequence of the object and the object is a consequence of the subject

as the distinction between subject and object is dissolved in the embrace of lovers whose discrete selves dissolve on a tide of sensation

in love the self embraces the otherness of the other but the other remains unknown

in lyric the poem embraces the feelingness of feeling but the feeling remains unknown

the feeling is the secret of the poem just as the otherness of the other is the other's secret

feeling may only exist in its other presents when it resonates within the present of the person who reads the poem this resonance occurs independently of the conscious desire of the reader or the writer of the poem

a relationship of power is negated in the lyric

being negated it is simultaneously asserted

the assertion of power in a lyric is the assertion of the power of feeling

it is a tautology, just as the statement 'I love you' is a tautology

lyric is radically redundant

**10**

lyric is berated for its lack of reality

although it is precisely its artifice which permits it to be real and precisely its lack of reality which permits it to be courteous towards reality

it is blamed for its sentiment

as if the conditions of feeling were understood enough to bypass their denials

it is condemned for its exclusions

despite its invitation to the present to open up to the world it is dismissed for its beauty

as if beauty were a dimension which did not belong to everything

it is attacked for its glorification of the self

although lyric doesn't have a self

it is the least commodity

because one cannot consume a condition of feeling

lyric can redeem and explain nothing

it is no consolation

it is useless

**11**

Nevertheless

# Notes on the poems

## Amplitudes

p40   *Gerard's Herbal* by John Gerard (1597)
p47   *The Emperor's Tomb* by Joseph Roth (1938).

## Specula

Specula is a three-part investigation into the writings of Mediaeval women mystics that consists of a poem, an essay and a radio play.

The essay was delivered at the Centre for Contemporary Poetics at Royal Holloway University of London and published by How2. It can be read online at https://www.asu.edu/pipercwcenter/how2journal/archive/online_archive/v2_2_2004/current/in_conference/croggon.htm.

The radio play, with music composed by Sam Mallet, was commissioned and broadcast by ABC Radio National in 2006.

The poem sections titled *Of Margery of Kempe* are drawn from the 15$^{th}$ century text *The Book of Margery Kempe*.

p264   Jacques de Vitry, quoted in *Woman Defamed and Woman Defended: An Anthology of Medieval Texts*, edited by Alcuin Blamires
p268   The Lingua Ignota was a divine language invented by the 12$^{th}$ century abbess and mystic Hildegard of Bingen.
p271   Jacques de Vitry, *The Life of Marie of Oignies*, 1233

www.ingramcontent.com/pod-product-compliance
Ingram Content Group UK Ltd.
Pitfield, Milton Keynes, MK11 3LW, UK
UKHW041304180426
11947UKWH00009B/686